AMERICA
UNDER ATTACK

Bible prophecy will help you understand
the treason in our country.

GERALD FLURRY

1ST EDITION
1st printing: March 2013, 15,000 copies
2nd printing: May 2013, 20,000 copies
3rd printing: May 2014, 15,000 copies
4th printing: July 2016, 15,000 copies
5th printing: August 2020, 10,000 copies

2ND EDITION
6th printing: June 2022, 25,000 copies
7th printing: August 2022, 10,000 copies

3RD EDITION
8th printing: March 2023, 25,000 copies

Scriptures in this publication are quoted from
the King James Version, unless otherwise noted.

Cover: Melissa Barreiro/PCG

CONTENTS

THE 'SWOONING' MEDIA

ACROSS THE GLOBE, PEOPLE ARE ASKING THE SAME QUESTION: *What has happened to the United States of America?* In just a few short years, the wealthiest, most powerful, most influential single nation in human history has become dangerously radicalized, divided and weak. It has rapidly fallen into political dysfunction, social division, economic woe, judicial and legislative compromise, and catastrophic moral failure. The nation Abraham Lincoln called "the last best hope of Earth" is, as he warned, about to "die by suicide."

Why? *Why* is the nation with every historic, geographical, cultural, economic and military advantage *destroying itself?*

This book, unlike any other, will reveal the core reason. It is *totally unseen* by most people in America and around the world.

This nation is committing suicide at the hands of certain powerful people in government and in society. They are actively, intentionally sabotaging this special nation *from the inside.* These radical elites have rapidly and fundamentally transformed American politics, governance, diplomacy, policing, morality, race, sex, tradition and culture.

This is what makes America's collapse so shocking, so historic and so excruciating: THE NATION IS BEING ATTACKED FROM WITHIN BY ITS OWN LEADERS.

How can you explain this? You need to know. As America falls, terrifying new powers are filling the void. The world is becoming a prey for autocratic states like Russia, China and Iran. America's self-destruction has already destabilized the world, increasing the dangers for all peoples—and this trend is certain to grow far worse.

This book will show you the REAL CAUSE for this crisis.

The Bible actually *prophesied* what is now happening in America. It describes it as "bitter affliction." This book exposes the cause of this affliction. It is the *only* book that does so.

The Bible also prophesies that God will *save* America from this affliction, in a specific way, through a specific man. This book gives you advance news of how God will relieve this bitterness soon, giving America its last chance at survival.

Understanding these truths supplies invaluable perspective amid the storms battering America. When you see the *cause,* then you can discern the real *solutions*—and you can have genuine hope in America's future.

AMERICA'S 'SWOONING' PRESS

It is difficult to understand this spiritual dimension. We cannot see it with our eyes, but we can certainly see its effects.

Let me give you a stunning example that occurred in 2013. I wrote about this in a booklet I published that year, also titled *America Under Attack.* That booklet was only 36 pages, but it vividly exposed the unseen cause of America's crisis. Events have since proved that booklet true, which is why I believe it needed to be expanded significantly into the book you are now reading.

In his book *Panic 2012: The Sublime and Terrifying Inside Story of Obama's Final Campaign,* author Michael Hastings described the captivating effect Barack Obama had on the journalists covering him during his second presidential campaign. Hastings told MSNBC's Martin Bashir, "That's THE PRESENCE OF OBAMA, even on the press corps—even on the people who follow him every day. When they're near him, they LOSE THEIR MINDS sometimes. THEY START BEHAVING IN WAYS THAT ARE JUVENILE, AND AMATEURISH, AND THEY *SWOON"* (emphasis mine throughout book).

What is that about? Reporters swooning and acting like nervous teenagers around a politician is *not normal.* I have never seen anything like it in American politics!

This is a damning indictment against our media. These journalists have a critical responsibility to find out the truth and inform the public. With Mr. Obama, they instead routinely gave fawning coverage. The mainstream media were practically *bewitched.* To this day, many journalists accept and promote what this man says even when it is provably false.

Hastings himself admitted to getting caught up in this behavior. He described an opportunity he had to interview Obama. "Did I ask the hardball questions? No, I did not," he admitted with a smile. Instead he asked "soft" questions. Bashir asked if he swooned around Obama. "I do," Hastings laughed. "I totally—oh man!"

This journalist thought this was funny. Was it really funny? Journalists acting this way toward a politician like Barack Obama is a colossal disaster!

Think deeply about this revelation from Hastings (who died a few months later). It is powerful evidence of the core problem afflicting America—a problem that has since grown significantly worse. Because the media swooned over President Obama, he was never held accountable. He was able to amass enormous power to do virtually *whatever he willed to do.* The media were simply unwilling to challenge him.

These journalists didn't even do their job during Obama's *first* presidential campaign in 2008. This contest for the nation's most powerful office came at a crucial time in our history, yet many of Mr. Obama's dangerous beliefs were unknown to the public before they voted for him. Why? Days before the election, prominent newsmen Tom Brokaw and Charlie Rose admitted that THE PRESS NEVER DID VET BARACK OBAMA. THEY FAILED TO CONDUCT A RIGOROUS EVALUATION OF THIS MAN. They gave him a pass and ignored deeply concerning evidence of his radical roots—evidence we will show you in this book.

On Election Night in 2008, MSNBC's Chris Matthews said, "The feeling most people get when they hear Barack Obama speak ... I felt this thrill going up my leg." What happens when the press becomes so spellbound? What could be more dangerous? Without a free and truthful media, a republic cannot survive!

Because the journalists swooned, because they avoided asking difficult questions, because they made a HERO out of Barack Obama, THIS MAN TOOK THE HIGHEST OFFICE IN THE LAND—TWICE.

What you need to see is that a DANGEROUS SPIRIT was at work here. There is a *powerful spiritual force* behind such inexplicable behavior. And in the years since, it has grown far stronger.

'THE GOD OF THIS WORLD'

With evil increasing in our world, I have seen more and more commentators talking about the fact that there is a spiritual dimension to human life. A number have openly acknowledged the existence of God. Some have even said American politics are being influenced by the devil. They likely do not realize how right they are.

Some people will scoff at what I am about to write, but it is absolutely true. You can prove it from your Bible.

2 Corinthians 4:4 calls Satan the devil "the god of this world." What does that mean? To say that he is this world's *god* means *he rules*—and people in this world *worship* him! It means this evil spirit being has FRIGHTENING POWER—power we can hardly imagine. This might sound extreme, but in these extreme and confusing times, doesn't it at least warrant consideration? There is a lot at stake for America, and for you personally.

This biblical truth explains the prevalence of evil around us. This is a crucial truth, and you need to prove it for yourself. (Our book *Mystery of the Ages,* by the late educator and theologian Herbert W. Armstrong, explains it with thorough scriptural proof. We will gladly send you a free copy.)

One of the Bible's most remarkable passages that show us the extent of the devil's power is in the book of Revelation. Revelation 12 describes an end-time war in heaven where great angelic beings fought against the devil and his demons, of which there are millions. Here is the outcome of that spiritual war: "[T]he dragon [Satan] fought and his angels [the *fallen* angels—the demons], And prevailed not; neither was their place found any more in heaven. And the great dragon was cast out, that old serpent, called the Devil, and SATAN, WHICH DECEIVETH THE WHOLE WORLD: he was cast out into the earth, and his angels were cast out with him" (verses 7-9).

Notice: Verse 9 says Satan *deceives the whole world*—everybody! His deception affects this world's education, its religion, its politics, its science—everything. So says your Bible.

Ephesians 2:2 calls Satan "the prince of the power of the air, the spirit that now worketh in the children of disobedience." The devil is stirring up people's emotions, moods and attitudes. When people get into a negative emotion or bad attitude, he works on those people even more. He has power to influence those wrong emotions; he has deceived the *world* through them! People don't understand God's Word—they lack spiritual depth—so they simply follow along emotionally, and Satan deceives them.

Revelation 12:9 is also an end-time prophecy. The book of Revelation puts all prophecy into a time sequence. That means you can know when the prophecy will be fulfilled. If you don't understand Revelation, you cannot understand Bible prophecy.

This verse tells us that Satan and the fallen angels—*millions* of demons—were driven out of heaven and cast down to Earth and are now CONFINED HERE! Never before has this world been so infested with demons. Look around: The evil proliferating in every direction has a source, and this prophecy exposes it.*

---

* For an explanation of when this event occurred, read Appendix B: "The Devil Cast Down."

WHY SATAN ATTACKS AMERICA

We are now living in this brief period when Satan is full of his worst wrath ever. Revelation 12:12 shows that he is infuriated because he knows his time of ruling Earth is almost over. This is woeful news in the short term, but a sign of *wonderful* news in the long term!

This book focuses on how Satan is attacking *America.* It reveals how he is using human beings—one in particular—to do so.

Why is the devil mounting such a dedicated offensive against this one nation? The answer reveals something profound, even inspiring.

America has been the world's most powerful country for most of the last century. It took over leadership from Britain, which was the greatest empire in history for the century before that. These two powers have occupied an utterly unique place in history, possessing unparalleled wealth and influence and using it in a way that benefited untold *billions* of people.

Our peoples tend to take credit for this spectacular success. But the truth is that *God gave us* these incomparable blessings.

Do you know why? It was not because of our righteousness or worthiness to receive them. Believe it or not, God bestowed these blessings to fulfill promises He had made *millenniums ago*—promises recorded in the Bible.

Yes, the history of these nations traces directly back to the pages of the Bible! This too is a truth you can prove.

Here is another truth you can prove: Most of the prophecies in the Bible are intended for the end time. The Prophet Daniel, for example, didn't even understand what he recorded. He was told to preserve it until it would be unsealed at "the time of the end" (Daniel 12:4, 8-9). The Prophet Isaiah also knew his message was for a time far after his own. God told him, "Now go, write it before them in a table, and note it in a book, that it may be for *the time to come* [meaning 'the latter day'] *for ever and ever*" (Isaiah 30:8). The Prophet Ezekiel was commissioned to warn "the children of Israel" of impending captivity—yet the Israelites had been conquered and taken captive years before. Like Daniel, Isaiah and the words of other prophets, his writings were recorded and miraculously preserved for thousands of years because the warning was intended for the *modern descendants* of ancient Israel.

There are many such prophecies in the Bible. However, the key that unlocks the meaning of so much biblical prophecy is widely unknown.

That all-important key is the identity of the descendants of Israel today.

The Bible is a book about God's chosen nation Israel and how God established it—despite the fact that its people were no better than other peoples—to serve as a blessing to all other nations. As Herbert W. Armstrong meticulously proved in his book *The United States and Britain in Prophecy,* the modern descendants of the biblical Israelites are in fact the American and British peoples! America's blessings are indeed *birthright* blessings that God promised the descendants of Abraham, Isaac and Israel—specifically those of Joseph's sons Ephraim and Manasseh (modern-day Britain and America; e.g. 1 Chronicles 5:2). End-time prophecy about *Israel* actually reveals the fate of the United States and Britain! (I urge you to request from us a free copy of *The United States and Britain in Prophecy.* Look in the back of the book for how to contact us.)

God prophesied of our power and prosperity. He also warned, throughout the Bible, that He would *remove* His blessing and protection if we rebelled. These nations enjoyed the fulfillment of the first part of those prophecies. They then rebelled against God. Now we are experiencing the *bitter affliction* of the latter part.

And at the same time that God has removed His protection, Satan and his demons are at their fiercest wrath! They hate God and everything He represents. Throughout history, they have concentrated their vilest attacks on God's chosen people. In this end time they are especially wrathful toward the most powerful of the modern Israelite nations: the United States of America.

God's ambition is to use Israel to set an example for all humanity. The big goal of the devil and his demons is to BRING ISRAEL DOWN. As we will see, they want to blot out even the *name* of Israel!

Evidence of the devil's success is all around us. That is the real story of the political, social and moral transformation of America. Satan has been influencing the minds of the elites in particular, increasingly steering policy and shaping public discourse. The mainstream media have been overcome by the devil. This has influenced millions of people. NEVER HAS ANYTHING LIKE THIS HAPPENED BEFORE. NEVER HAVE AMERICANS SEEN SUCH A SATANIC ABERRATION IN THEIR PRESIDENTIAL POLITICS.

2 Corinthians 11:14 reveals that "Satan himself is transformed into an angel of light." He is skilled at deceit and intimidation, and he is using these powers to conquer this nation.

That is what the Michael Hastings example is all about. By Mr. Obama's second term, Satan had all the mainstream media "swooning"! THE REPORTERS SWOONED AS THE DEVIL TOOK CONTROL OF THE COUNTRY.

This book tells the full story of how Satan has gotten a stranglehold on America. And as you will see, he has done so by using *one man*—a man with such arrogance that he opened himself up to terrible satanic influence.

This book also shows how God *confronted* the attack on America that took place during President Obama's two terms. It reveals the crucial role Donald Trump fulfilled, a role also prophesied in the Bible. It provides spiritual perspective on the presidency of Joe Biden, who is effectively a front man for a third Obama term. And it gives you the stunning revelation— made plain in prophecy—of how this satanic attack will be STOPPED.

Prophecy shows that Mr. Trump's role in U.S. politics is *not over.* But what happens when he returns to power will shock you.

It is critical to see the devil's influence in what is happening. But you must also see God's hand. This gives you wonderful perspective, even amid some of the darkest days our nation has ever faced. Knowing why God is allowing this, and how He plans to use these events to ultimately bless every American and every other human being, will give you unsurpassed vision and hope!

CHAPTER ONE

BARACK OBAMA— 'FUNDAMENTALLY TRANSFORMING AMERICA'

Januar 20, 2017, was Barack Obama's last day in the Oval Office. That day, he left a handwritten message for the incoming president, Donald Trump. He wrote that America's presidents are "guardians of those democratic institutions and traditions—like rule of law, separation of powers, equal protection and civil liberties—that our forebears fought and bled for. Regardless of the push and pull of daily politics, it's up to us to leave those instruments of our democracy at least as strong as we found them."

Mr. Obama's note seemed noble and sincere. It was treated as such by many politicians and journalists. But it is one of the most diabolical and hypocritical messages ever written by an American president.

Barack Obama spent his eight years as president doing exactly the opposite of what he told Mr. Trump: advancing his agenda to *weaken* those democratic institutions and traditions in pursuit of his supreme stated goal of "fundamentally transforming the United States of America."

After leaving office, Mr. Obama continued to pursue this goal. He spearheaded the effort to harm Donald Trump's "Make America Great Again" agenda, an effort that included illegally spying on him and impeaching him twice. He directed the radical left's treasonous battle to prevent Mr. Trump from being reelected at all costs.

The United States entered its greatest political crisis ever on November 3, 2020, Election Day. To make Joe Biden president, the radical left flagrantly manipulated the nation's voting system.

Initially, the mainstream media, perhaps half the citizens, most of the nation's politicians (Democrats *and* Republicans), and much of the rest of the world believed or at least behaved as though Mr. Biden had been legitimately elected president by the official total of 81 million votes.

But it was a giant lie. Mountains of evidence prove that the election was manipulated. At court hearings in several states, hundreds of witnesses gave firsthand accounts of widespread election fraud. Thousands of witnesses signed affidavits attesting to it. Scientists and data analysts investigated the numbers and testified of the statistical impossibility of some of the official vote counts. Electronic voting machines and software were audited and revealed dishonest activity. Security video footage and cell phone geolocation data showed ballot "mules" stuffing drop boxes with stacks of ballots, sometimes in the middle of the night. Many of these people hid their identity with masks, obscured their fingerprints with disposable gloves, and photographed themselves with the ballots at the drop boxes to ensure they received payment for their crimes.[*]

The 2020 election was hacked, and it reduced America's entire electoral system to shambles. And it is all because of the radical left's unrestrained assault on America's "democratic institutions and traditions," INCLUDING THE CONSTITUTION AND THE RULE OF LAW. Thousands of people and institutions were directly or indirectly involved. Virtually all of America's top media organizations and personalities were complicit, as well as the powerful tech companies and many of the nation's top politicians.

---

[*] There is more information about the 2020 election steal in Chapter 8.

But this vast network of lies, corruption and lawlessness all points back to one man: Barack Obama.

As we will see, this epic scandal would not have taken place if not for Obama's leadership of the Democratic Party and the radical left. And THERE IS PROOF THAT HE NOT ONLY WAS AWARE OF THE PLOT TO PERVERT THE 2020 ELECTION BUT WAS DIRECTLY OR INDIRECTLY LEADING THOSE PULLING THE STRINGS.

Many have referred to this as a *rolling coup*—an ongoing insurgence against American constitutional government—and they are right. This coup was initiated by Barack Obama *before* he left office in January 2017. *Even as he was writing that "beautiful" message instructing Donald Trump to guard democracy and the rule of law,* THIS MAN WAS DEVISING PLANS TO OVERTHROW MR. TRUMP AND RETURN THE RADICAL LEFT TO THE WHITE HOUSE!

I want to show how the 2020 election crisis exposes Mr. Obama and his closest allies. After Election Day, the corruption in America's politics and electoral system was dramatically uncovered. This exposed a startling lurch toward lawlessness in this nation.

More importantly, this crisis reveals the unseen but potent force *behind* Mr. Obama and the radical left, and it spotlights a crucial biblical prophecy. To understand Barack Obama, the 2020 election and America's immediate future, you need to understand that prophecy.

Before we examine that evidence, however, let's look further back in the story.

Barack Obama is unlike any other president America has ever had. His public persona has been shaped by his three memoirs, which the media have accepted at face value. But there are many disturbing truths about his childhood and early adulthood that he does not mention in these autobiographies that should have been known and examined when the American people were considering him for the nation's most powerful office. It is amazing how much about his life was concealed or distorted by the media before he became president. It's as if Americans were *not allowed* to know the man who was about to be their leader.

A TRAGIC CHILDHOOD

Obama's story is tragic in many ways. His biological father was a womanizer from Kenya whom he met only once and who abandoned him when he was a young child. Years later, his mother also abandoned him, leaving him with his grandparents. He had a very sad childhood. He was a vulnerable and emotionally neglected boy. He was confused and angry, in search of father and mother figures.

In his biography *Rising Star: The Making of Barack Obama*, David Garrow writes that in 1970, when Obama was 9 or 10 years old, his mother hired "an openly gay 24-year-old, sometimes-cross-dressing man ... to be both cook and nanny." This babysitter tried to avoid letting the young Obama see him in women's clothes, but he would try on makeup in front of him.

During his teen years, Obama's mother lived in Indonesia, and he lived with his grandparents in Hawaii. Garrow notes that Obama's main challenges growing up had nothing to do with race; Hawaii is one of the most culturally diverse places in America. Most of Obama's friends from high school describe Obama's anger as having more to do with the lack of parental attention. One of his close friends said, "Obama's parents were a 'total and complete mystery.' Obama never spoke about them, he recalled: 'I knew nothing about his father, and I can't say that I knew he had a mother at all.'"

During his junior year of high school, Obama was a member of the "Choom Gang," a Hawaiian slang term for smoking marijuana. It was known that Obama smoked marijuana, but the media have downplayed how heavily he used this drug during his preparatory years. He and his friends smoked marijuana almost daily and, when they could afford it, experimented with cocaine and heroin.

The group's drug dealer was a homosexual named Ray Boyer. Obama and his friends referred to him as "Gay Ray." Ray lived in a bus in an abandoned warehouse. He was also heavily into pornography. One of Obama's friends recalled that "Gay Ray" would get the boys high, then they would watch pornography together.

Obama's high school yearbook gave each graduating senior a quarter page to use as they wished. Obama's friends included references to their antics and memorialized the group by writing the initials of each member. On Obama's page, in addition to acknowledging his friends, he mentioned Ray. Garrow writes that Obama, "alone of all the Choom Gang, had singled out their weird, gay, porn-showing drug dealer by name and thanked him 'for all the good times.'"

It is appalling to surrender a young man to such destructive influences. The Bible describes a time in ancient Israel of such corruption that the people sacrificed their own children (e.g. 2 Kings 17:17; Psalm 106:37-38; Jeremiah 7:31; 19:5). How savage and barbaric! Yet we see parents doing effectively the same thing today: People are sacrificing their children morally, mentally and spiritually by turning them over to all sorts of evil influences. Whether they realize it or not, they are opening their children up to deadly attacks from the devil.

When someone has that kind of childhood, Satan can exploit that. The fruits strongly suggest that in the case of a young Barack Obama, he exploited it in a profound way.

RACISM, COMMUNISM

One of the most influential figures on young Obama was his maternal grandfather's black friend Frank Marshall Davis. Davis was literally a card-carrying Communist. He had been surveilled by the Federal Bureau of Investigation for several years in the 1940s and '50s. He was also a poet and a pornographer. Obama's grandfather encouraged him to talk with Davis one-on-one.

Davis focused Obama on the struggles of black Americans. He is largely responsible for developing Obama's views on race and racial identity.

The *American Spectator* printed an article about Davis, with the quip "Meet the hard-core Communist who mentored the future 44th president of the United States" (Oct. 12, 2012).

"In short, Frank Marshall Davis's writings were outrageous," Paul Kengor wrote. "A Jeremiah Wright sermon or Bill Ayers lecture is tame by comparison." Bill Ayers is a white American socialist terrorist and an associate of Mr. Obama.

Obama vaguely references Davis in his first autobiography, referring to him more than 20 times but only as "Frank"— references he later censored. He is conspicuously quiet about his meetings with Davis. When he started his political career decades later, his relationship with Davis would become a liability. Obama said the relationship was nothing and that he only met with him something like 15 times.

In 1980, Obama attended Occidental College in Los Angeles, California. During summer vacation, he returned to Hawaii and experienced another race-based turning point. Obama's white grandmother came home one afternoon after being frightened by a black homeless man while she was waiting for a bus. Obama sought Frank's advice on the matter. According to Obama, Frank told him, "[Y]our grandma's right to be scared. ... She understands that black people have a reason to hate. That's just how it is. For your sake, I wish it was otherwise. But it's not. So you might as well get used to it."

Obama says that upon reflecting on their conversation, "The earth shook under my feet, ready to crack open at any moment. I stopped, trying to steady myself, and knew for the first time that I was utterly alone" (*Dreams From My Father*).

It appears this talk awakened Obama's racial consciousness. Obama experienced no significant race-related problems growing up, but that didn't keep him from using race as a political tool later in life. Frank Marshall Davis was instrumental in fanning the flames of racial grievance and inspiring the racial agenda of the future president of the United States.

At Occidental College, Obama wrote, "To avoid being mistaken for a sellout, I chose my friends carefully. The more politically active black students. The foreign students. The Chicanos. The Marxist professors and structural feminists and punk-rock performance poets." OBAMA ADMITTED TO CHOOSING MARXIST PROFESSORS. "We smoked cigarettes and wore leather jackets. At night, in the dorms, we discussed neocolonialism, Franz [sic] Fanon, Eurocentrism and patriarchy. When we ground out our cigarettes in the hallway carpet or set our stereos so loud that the walls began to shake, we were resisting bourgeois society's stifling constraints. We weren't indifferent or careless or insecure. We were alienated." If I had done those things, I certainly wouldn't brag about them in a book.

One of Obama's professors was Lawrence Goldyn, who taught comparative politics. Goldyn was known on the Occidental campus for being its only openly homosexual professor. Garrow writes that many years later, when asked about his perspective on homosexual issues, Obama said, "My favorite professor my first year in college was one of the first openly gay people that I knew. ... He was a terrific guy." In later interviews, Obama discussed his "strong friendship" with Goldyn and admired how he displayed "comfort in his own skin." Garrow writes that he "wrote somewhat elusively to his first intimate girlfriend that he had thought about and considered gayness, but ultimately had decided that a same-sex relationship would be less challenging and demanding than developing one with the opposite sex."

In the fall of 1980, Obama accepted an invitation from a friend at Occidental, Mohammed Hasan Chandoo, to share a two-bedroom apartment. Garrow writes that during the academic year of 1980–81, Obama and Chandoo "became the closest of friends." "Marijuana was a regular though perhaps not nightly relaxant for Hasan and Barry," Garrow writes. Chandoo's girlfriend admitted that the group occasionally snorted cocaine. At one point he tried psychedelic mushrooms.

Though Obama later admitted to using drugs, he said it was minimal. Months before the 2008 presidential election, the *New York Times* published this headline: "Old Friends Say Drugs Played Bit Part in Obama's Young Life." The article said Obama's friends may have downplayed his drug use to protect his reputation.

Such drug use weakens the mind and makes a person more susceptible to damaging spiritual forces. Did these activities open this door within the life of the man who would become America's president?

TRANSFORMED PERSONA

Chandoo, a Pakistani with whom Obama "became the closest of friends," identified himself as a Marxist. Another friend remembered that he "was very radical at the time." During the fall semester of 1981, Obama became more politically active. He began attending Marxist rallies. Friends remember that Obama "argued a rather simple-minded version of Marxist theory" and that "he was passionate about his point of view." Obama and Chandoo started a chapter at the college of "the Committee in Solidarity With the People of El Salvador," a group that supported El Salvador's left-wing opposition, which had ties to the Communist party. Chandoo also organized a forum on campus featuring a former Pakistani Supreme Court justice and the exiled founder of Pakistan's militant Marxist party.

In *Dreams From My Father,* Obama describes a night when his white friends were polite but visibly uncomfortable at a party where most of the people were black. After that night, he wrote, "I had begun to see a new map of the world, one that was frightening in its simplicity, suffocating in its implications. ... [A]ny distinction between good and bad whites held negligible meaning. In fact, you couldn't even be sure that everything you had assumed to be an expression of your black, unfettered self ... had been freely chosen by you. At best, these things were a refuge; at worst, a trap. Following this maddening logic, the only thing you could choose as your own was withdrawal into a smaller and smaller coil of rage, until being black meant only the knowledge of your own powerlessness, of your own defeat. And the final irony: Should you refuse this defeat and lash out at your captors, they would have a name for that, too, a name that could cage you just as good. Paranoid. Militant. Violent. Ni***r. Over the next few months, I looked to corroborate this nightmare vision. [Reading books by Baldwin, Ellison, Hughes, Wright, DuBois and Malcolm X], trying to reconcile the world as I'd found it with the terms of my birth."

About this time, Garrow writes, "Obama also realized that the beer drinking, pot smoking and cocaine snorting that Oxy [Occidental College], like Punahou [Obama's preparatory high school], offered him, and that had cemented his reputation as a 'hard-core party animal' to some friends, was incompatible with any self-transformation into a more serious student and person."

Obama decided to remake himself. He wanted a fresh start. One friend recalled that Obama wanted to move somewhere where he would have "access to a black cultural experience that I don't actually know."

Obama transferred to Columbia University in New York City in 1982. There he went to stay with a friend of Chandoo's named Siddiqi. Garrow writes that "Siddiqi also witnessed a 'transformation' from the 'fun-loving ... easygoing' Obama he had met 18 months earlier in South Pasadena to someone who was now 'very serious and less lighthearted.'"

In an interview years later, Obama spoke about his time at Columbia. Garrow writes that his mother jokingly called him Gandhi "because of his newly ascetic life, but Barack did not deny that he had become 'deadly serious' during those late college years."

Obama recalled, "People would invite me to parties, and I'd say, 'What are you talking about? WE'VE GOT A REVOLUTION THAT HAS TO TAKE PLACE.'"

Barack Obama was now on a course that would lead him to the Democratic Party, Chicago, the Senate and the presidency.

ENTRY INTO POLITICS

After Columbia University, Obama moved to Chicago, where he entered the world of community organizing. He was looking for a place to belong and trying to create an identity for himself. He would forge one in Chicago. In a 2007 article for the *New Republic,* Ryan Lizza wrote that Obama "longed for an experience that connected him to the civil rights era." Obama wrote in his autobiography that he "earned" his membership in the African-American community "through organizing" and "shared sacrifice." Obama, Lizza wrote, "wanted to join the club."

Obama began attending church services under Pastor Jeremiah Wright. Decades later, his relationship with Wright would become one of the few challenges he would face in his political career. During his 2008 presidential campaign, clips of Wright's sermons began to surface on the Internet. These show WRIGHT'S ANGER AND INDIGNATION ("RACISM IS THE AMERICAN WAY!") DURING HIS PROFANITY-LADEN, CONSPIRACY-THEORY-BASED SCREEDS ("THE GOVERNMENT LIED ABOUT INVENTING THE HIV VIRUS AS A MEANS OF GENOCIDE AGAINST PEOPLE OF COLOR") cloaked in spiritual language ("Jesus was a poor black man ... who lived in a culture that was controlled by rich white people!"). IN THESE CLIPS, WRIGHT'S MOST SLANDEROUS STATEMENTS RECEIVE THE WILDEST CHEERS FROM HIS CONGREGATION.

BARACK OBAMA INSISTED THAT HE NEVER HEARD WRIGHT SAY THOSE THINGS. BUT HE ATTENDED THIS MAN'S ANTI-SEMITIC, ANTI-WHITE CHURCH FOR 20 YEARS. For two decades he sat in Wright's church hearing him rant malicious hate toward this country. Their relationship was deep. Obama titled one of his books *The Audacity of Hope,* after one of Wright's sermons.

Sadly, the press and much of the American public willingly overlooked this startling warning sign. It is as if they were in a stupor, UNCONCERNED THAT OBAMA'S WORLDVIEW WAS SHAPED BY SOME OF THE MOST RADICAL AND RACIST MINDS IN AMERICA!

While in Chicago, Obama learned about the Saul Alinsky approach to community organizing. In his book *Rules for Radicals,* Alinsky praised Lucifer for being the "first radical known to man who rebelled against the establishment and did it so effectively that he at least won his own kingdom." Obama never met Alinsky personally, but he was trained by some of Alinsky's closest followers.

"Alinsky had been dead for more than a decade when Obama arrived in Chicago, but his legacy was still very much alive," Lizza wrote about Obama's connection to the man. "[Mike] Kruglik, [Gerald] Kellman and [Gregory] Galluzzo had all studied his teachings through the Industrial Areas Foundation (IAF), the organizing school Alinsky founded. By the '80s, not even the IAF strictly adhered to every principle that Alinsky taught. But at least one of Obama's teachers considered himself a true believer: 'I regard myself as St. Paul who never met Jesus,' Galluzzo told me of Alinsky, who died shortly after Galluzzo moved to Chicago on a pilgrimage to meet him in 1972. 'I'm his best disciple.'"

Galluzzo was one of three men who taught Obama about community organizing.

Obama left Chicago to attend Harvard. But, as Lizza noted, Obama "kept a foot in the world of organizing." Obama traveled to Los Angeles to attend a training course taught by the IAF. Lizza wrote that after Harvard, Obama returned to Chicago where "he served on the boards of both the Woods Fund and the Joyce Foundation, which also gives grants to Alinsky-style groups, and continued to teach organizing workshops."

After attending the University of Chicago, Obama went into state politics in Illinois, first as a state senator in 1996 and then eight years in the U.S. Senate. In just 12 years, Obama went from being a little-known state politician to president of the United States of America. Few politicians move that swiftly through the ranks of politics.

Throughout Obama's political career, almost nobody would talk about these damaging influences on his youth, his final meeting with Frank that shook the earth under his feet, his time at Occidental, his new sense of purpose, the solidifying of his racial agenda, and his transformation into a revolutionary. They overlooked how these factors influenced Barack Obama's view of this nation. And they failed to connect these facts to his declaration during a rally on October 30, 2008, just prior to the 2008 presidential election: "We are five days away from fundamentally transforming the United States of America."

Barack Obama wanted to fundamentally transform the nation because he disagreed with its founding principles. He believed that the Constitution was created *by* rich white people *for* rich white people and that whites have been stealing from everyone else. He was deeply sympathetic to an ideology that directly, even violently, opposes America's constitutional government: communism.

FUNDAMENTAL TRANSFORMATION

As president, Mr. Obama passionately pursued his ambition to transform America. And he found formidable success.

Let's start with one example. Many people said that electing (and reelecting) a black man to the most powerful office in the world would solve our nation's racial problems. It did the opposite. That is because Barack Obama actively fomented those problems.

President Obama repeatedly made public remarks on racially charged issues, remarks that increased people's mistrust of the police and eroded faith in the justice system. He said things that were provably false but that played well to racist radicals.* *At one point Obama said racism is part of America's* DNA. *That means the nation is* IRREDEEMABLY *racist.* SUCH A BASELESS ACCUSATION IS SATANIC TO ITS CORE! Satan uses race as a weapon to divide people. God doesn't hold any race as superior or inferior to any other; He made all races and has a transcendent potential in store for all people!

In the post-Obama America, mainstream media and radical Democrats continually accuse Republicans and everyday

---

* You can read about these instances in Chapter 5 of my free booklet *Great Again.* That booklet is a good companion read to this book.

Americans of being racist. In almost every case, they are lying and they *know* they're lying. Radicals *encourage* racism against whites, teaching white students—even elementary schoolchildren—to think they are inferior to blacks, Hispanics and anybody of color. We frequently hear racist remarks on television and radio. One black TV commentator on NBC said, "This is no country for young black men!" Such ugly, racist remarks are filling the country with hatred and division that will lead to violence and race war. These commentators are either ignorant of what they are doing, or they *want* a race war. Certainly some extremists do. BIBLE PROPHECY TELLS US THEY ARE GOING TO GET ONE.

This is just one example of how Barack Obama transformed America. There are many more.

The Obama administration deceitfully forced through the Affordable Care Act, a destructive piece of legislation that increased national debt and made America more of a socialist state. It permitted the Internal Revenue Service to illegally target conservative groups through audits, bank account seizures, surveillance and other forms of harassment. This was one of many ways that, under Obama, federal institutions were politicized and weaponized. Later chapters in this book detail how this dangerous process was particularly egregious with the Federal Bureau of Investigation, the Central Intelligence Agency and other intelligence agencies. President Obama used these and other federal institutions to spy on American senators and representatives, journalists, political campaigns and millions of everyday Americans. These actions seriously eroded the rule of law, undermined constitutional protections for the American people, and pushed the country dramatically toward tyranny.

The Obama administration perpetrated equally major "fundamental changes" in America's foreign policy. In 2009, President Obama visited Cairo, Egypt, and gave a speech aimed at reconciling with Iran. He said nobody had the right to deny nuclear weapons to this terrorist-sponsoring nation. This speech helped to provoke, and the Obama administration supported, a popular Islamist uprising against Egyptian President Hosni Mubarak (a good friend of Israel), which brought the Muslim Brotherhood into power. Then his government ignored the popular revolt in Iran, strengthening the radical mullahs in the number one terrorist-sponsoring nation in the world. Then it negotiated a grotesque nuclear deal with the Iranian leaders, freeing Iranian spies, flooding Iran with cash, and providing a lifeline for ongoing nuclear activity. And when a jihadist mob attacked America's embassy in Benghazi, Libya, on the anniversary of 9/11 in 2012, and terrorists killed an ambassador and three other Americans, Obama officials shamefully told our people to *stand down*. They then tried to deflect blame for the killings away from the killers and apologized for America supposedly provoking the attack.*

On several occasions, Obama insulted Britain and displayed hostility toward the Jewish state. Yet he restored diplomatic ties with Cuba, rescuing its Communist government and giving powerful enemies a path to pressure and threaten America from less than 100 miles away. He enthusiastically supported international organizations like the corrupt World Health Organization and the anti-Israel, anti-American United Nations. He eagerly participated in the Paris Climate Accords, which strangled America's industry and economy.

Such pernicious actions characterized everything Barack Obama did as president. We will study more deeply into several of them in this book. These are the actions of a man and his cabal "fundamentally transforming" a nation he viewed as fundamentally evil.

Yet the truth is, Barack Obama was used as a tool by a spirit being with *far greater* hatred of America.

Most people will not talk about this, but it is the truth, and only the truth will make us free (John 8:32; 17:17).

---

* More on these foreign-policy disasters in Chapters 6 and 9.

ANTIOCHUS

Most people say they believe the Bible. I would like you to think about the example recorded in 1 Samuel 16:14 and 19:9-10 of King Saul of Israel, who was troubled by an evil spirit and tried to kill the man God chose to replace him.

Do you believe it is possible that an evil spirit could influence the king of Israel? It has happened—a number of times.

The Apostle Paul made a profound statement in 2 Corinthians 2:11. He said that we had better not be ignorant of the devices of the devil, or else we will become his victims.

The devil is real. THE DEVIL LIVES! People scoff, but they won't be scoffing long. They will soon realize how ignorant they were of Satan's devices and wiles.

Many historical and prophetic biblical passages show how Satan works through human beings, particularly through men in positions of power. One stunning and detailed example appears in the eighth chapter of the book of Daniel.

Daniel's prophecy is *specifically* for this end time—and for no other time (Daniel 12:4, 9). The last part of Daniel 8:17 reads, "Understand, O son of man, that the vision *is for the time of the end*" (Revised Standard Version). In verse 26, God told Daniel to seal up the vision, "for it relates to the FAR FUTURE" (Moffatt). Many of the events described in this chapter were fulfilled *in type* in the centuries after Daniel recorded them in 550 B.C. However, even those events point to this prophecy's *primary* fulfillment, which occurs in the END TIME, the final years of the age of man just before the Second Coming of Jesus Christ.

Beginning in verse 9 is a prophecy of a "little horn" that arose from one of the four divisions of the Grecian Empire. Virtually all commentaries agree this was a prophecy of Antiochus IV Epiphanes, a deceptive, wicked Seleucid king who obtained rule in Palestine in 176 B.C. through deceit and flattery.

While peoples in other areas were allowed to keep their religions, Antiochus wrathfully destroyed many Jewish men, women and children, and tried to destroy the Jewish faith itself.

He robbed the temple, set up a pagan altar and an idol of himself inside it, murdered or enslaved tens of thousands of Jews in Jerusalem, and burned and demolished much of the city.

This man was clearly heavily influenced if not possessed by the devil, who used him for shockingly destructive ends. We will study more into this historical example later in the book.

Commentaries acknowledge Daniel's prophecy was fulfilled in the second century B.C. What they do not understand is that this "little horn" prophecy also has an *end-time* fulfillment, which is most important. Again, Daniel's prophecy is for the end time—our time today.

The end-time fulfillment of this prophecy is detailed and significant, and I explain it in my booklets *Daniel—Unsealed at Last!* and *Daniel Unlocks Revelation* (request your free copies). This prophecy is ultimately speaking of a leader in Europe who will unite a terrifying European empire that will attack America and the other modern-day nations of Israel.

What I will show you in this book, however, is the evidence that America has been ruled *from within* by another type of Antiochus. For eight years, this man used deceit and flattery as he sabotaged the nation from the top of our own government! I realize this is an explosive claim, but the evidence is abundant. Daniel's prophecy provides extraordinary insight into our nation's political crisis.

I have been warning about Mr. Obama and his anti-American ambitions since before he became president. During his presidency, I explained that he was an Antiochus-type who sought the destruction of our constitutional republic. This was the main theme of my much smaller 2013 booklet *America Under Attack.*

When Mr. Obama left the White House in January 2017, some said this was a failed prophecy. He was no longer president, and it appeared he had little influence on American politics, especially as his successor tried to undo much of his work. But as you will read in this book, the truth is that this Antiochus never left the political scene. Even after leaving the White House, he continued working his agenda. And he has never stopped trying to undermine America.

Barack Obama came as an "angel of light," and millions of Americans believed and still believe him. But as president, was he the guardian of America's "democratic institutions and traditions—like rule of law"? Did he leave the "instruments of our democracy at least as strong as [he] found them"?

HE DID PRECISELY THE OPPOSITE. Focus on his ACTIONS. Look at his FRUITS. Anybody should be able to see past the "angelic" artifice and recognize the real power at work. HIS FRUITS DEFINE WHAT HE MEANT BY "FUNDAMENTALLY TRANSFORMING AMERICA."

Abraham Lincoln was perhaps the greatest president America ever had. He said, "I am nothing, but TRUTH IS EVERYTHING." Lincoln received that understanding from the Bible (e.g. John 8:31-32; 2 Thessalonians 2:10). God helped us through men like Lincoln, who believed the truth is everything.

What happens, however, if the people and their leaders don't believe that? What if you believe and follow and propagate lies? Then you are following the "father of lies."

That makes Barack Obama a very dangerous man!

CHAPTER TWO

LAW UNDER ATTACK

I N September 2012, constitutional experts presented a list to the House Judiciary Committee showing how President Obama was exceeding the legal constraints of the presidency during his first term. *HumanEvents.com* summarized the panel's findings this way: "As president, Barack Obama has made a habit of bypassing or ignoring constitutional limitations on his power ...." Examples included his abuse of executive power in connection with the Fast and Furious scandal, his decision to stop enforcing parts of America's immigration law, and his authorization of military action in Libya in 2011 without first consulting Congress.

One of the panel's main examples was Obama's 2012 unilateral appointments of officials, bypassing Senate confirmation. A federal court ruled that this was unconstitutional. "Sen. Mike Lee, ... a noted constitutional scholar, told the committee that Obama's abuse of power ... was a HISTORIC FIRST" (ibid). This had never happened in U.S. history.

Barack Obama's administration routinely pushed past the limits of executive power. The *New York Times* wrote in April 2012, "[I]ncreasingly in recent months, the administration has been seeking WAYS to *act without Congress.*" Even the president's allies in the media knew this was happening. But nobody did anything to stop it. Few people were even paying attention!

It has since become clear how much Obama and his people took advantage of this lack of vigilance.

Do you realize how deadly dangerous this trend of lawlessness is? Very few people do. But it gives profound insight into the real nature of the threat facing America today. America's Constitution makes this nation different from any other in the world. It is based on biblical principles. The protections afforded by the Constitution have allowed God to bless this nation tremendously. They prevent a dictator from seizing control of the nation's unmatched resources—resources God gave us.

The Constitution was one of many blessings that made America the greatest nation in history. God has blessed America like no other nation. And the devil wants to destroy America like no other nation! Satan is marshaling every weapon he can to wreck America, and he is having alarming success.

Again, biblical prophecy supplies crucial insight into why.

CASTING TRUTH TO THE GROUND

Look again at the prophecy of Daniel 8. It describes Satan's activities in a very telling way. It applies in principle to what has happened to America.

Beginning in verse 10 is a description of an attack Satan made in this end time. The prophetic language here references God's "sanctuary" and the "daily sacrifice," using the temple of God in ancient Israel as a prophetic symbol. This describes a satanic assault on the modern "sanctuary," God's Church. Still, it exposes the devil's tactics in his assault on the United States as well.*

Verse 12 says the devil had a "host," speaking of an *army* of his demons: "And an host was given him against the daily sacrifice

---

* To understand this requires study, but you can grasp the point as it relates to America without such study. If you want further explanation, read Appendix A: "Prophetic Duality." I also explain the spiritual fulfillment of these verses in Daniel 8 in my free booklet *Daniel—Unsealed at Last!*

by reason of transgression, and IT CAST DOWN THE TRUTH TO THE GROUND; and it practised, and prospered."

Satan is always working to CAST THE TRUTH TO THE GROUND. God is a God of truth. His word is truth. His law is true and right, and keeping it makes our lives happy, orderly and blessed. His way is the way of goodness, righteousness, law and order (e.g. John 17:17; Psalm 19:7-9; 119:151; 1 Corinthians 14:40).

A truthful, law-abiding society, even keeping man-made laws, is far more stable than a lawless one.

Satan, the god of this world, is a deceiver. He is a liar and the father of liars (John 8:44). He hates truth. He relishes lawlessness and disorder (although he also inspires tyranny and authoritarianism, which use law not as a blessing to people but as a weapon against them). He always sways people to disparage and break the law; he undermines the rule of law. Once people do that, then he can send in his demons and wreak havoc—on an individual, a church or a nation.

When you see a spirit of deceit and lawlessness at work, you know the devil is behind that.

When Satan attacked God's Church in this end time, he got people in at the top who cast the truth to the ground. (This story is told in our free book *Raising the Ruins*. It is stunning history that parallels the destruction in America in remarkable ways.)

Satan has used the *same tactics* when attacking America and the modern-day nations of Israel. This explains the onslaught against America's founding, history, principles and purpose coming from such high-placed leaders. This is the most efficient and potent way to destroy: from the top down. The devil can use those leaders to wage an assault from within on the truth and the law.

THIS IS A CORE CHARACTERISTIC OF THE WORK OF A SATAN-INSPIRED "ANTIOCHUS." The Antiochus figure prophesied in Daniel 8 is a *lawless* man. He is unconstrained by the law of God, and even by the laws of man. Instead, he follows the dictates of his own will, which is, tragically, inspired by the devil.

EXECUTIVE ORDERS

In his State of the Union address in February 2013, President Obama said: "I urge this Congress to pursue a bipartisan, market-based solution to climate change .... *But if Congress won't act soon to protect future generations,* I WILL. I will direct my cabinet to come up with EXECUTIVE ACTIONS we can take, now and in the future ...."

Obama took these types of actions with unequaled frequency. Here is what the *Washington Post* wrote just a couple of days before the president's address: "President Obama is considering a series of new executive actions aimed at working around a recalcitrant Congress, including policies that could allow struggling homeowners to refinance their mortgages, provide new protections for gays and lesbians, make buildings more energy-efficient, and toughen regulations for coal-fired power plants .... The moves underscore Obama's *increasingly aggressive use of executive authority,* including 23 administrative actions on gun violence last month and previous orders that delayed deportations of young illegal immigrants and will lower student loan payments" (Feb. 10, 2013).

Such actions conditioned people's minds to accept executive orders that were primarily intended to *circumvent Congress and the Constitution.* THIS MOVED THE NATION DRAMATICALLY TOWARD RULE BY DICTATORSHIP OR TYRANNY.

President Obama's use of drones also illegally expanded his power. He launched five times more drone strikes than President George W. Bush did, and in half the time. One of these targeted and killed an American citizen in Yemen. Far more chilling was this: The Department of Justice leaked a 16-page document to NBC showing that Obama's administration assumed power to kill any American citizen it considered a threat, even on American soil. It plainly, boldly considered itself ABOVE THE LAW.

Judge Andrew Napolitano wrote in the *Washington Times:* "Obama has argued that he can kill Americans whose deaths he believes will keep us all safer, without any due process whatsoever. *No law authorizes that.* His attorney general has argued that the president's careful consideration of each target and the narrow use of deadly force are an adequate and constitutional substitute for due process. No court has ever approved that" (Feb. 7, 2013). Napolitano pointed out that this practice broke state and federal laws, executive orders prohibiting assassinations, language in the Declaration of Independence, and the Constitution.

Perhaps many or even most of the people targeted in these attacks *were* threats to the United States. But we should be deeply troubled by an administration so disdainful of the law that it is supposed to uphold!

This trend toward lawlessness is DEADLY. And because it was not forcibly stopped, this problem intensified throughout Obama's presidency. It is now even worse with Joe Biden in power. WE MUST OPEN OUR EYES TO RECOGNIZE THE EVIL SPIRITUAL FORCE THAT IS BEHIND THIS PUSH TO UNDERMINE THE LAW.

We in America have been protected for a couple hundred years because we are recipients of the blessings God promised to faithful Abraham. We have not experienced the turmoil that many other nations have. We were involved in a civil war and two world wars, but compared to most other countries and other eras, God has given us victories and a lot of peace. As a result, our people have settled into an *unreality* about what is happening around us. They don't understand how deadly dangerous it is!

This is not God's world. It is a world plagued by great evil. It is full of tigers waiting to tear people apart. As Winston Churchill said, the history of man is the HISTORY OF WAR. Yet somehow we can't come to grips with that today. It is so much easier to ignore it.

Are you willing to face reality? Most people are not. A haze of deception enshrouds our world. It is stunning how easily people are duped today.

I wonder how many Americans even know that the Constitution IS the supreme law of the land. It is similar to how the Ten Commandments is the supreme law of God and the foundation of the entire Bible. It works beautifully if you just apply it. But radical leftists *hate the supreme law of the land.*

Barack Obama has criticized the U.S. Constitution as "a charter of negative liberties" and called it outdated. Liberals in academia, the media and in government believe governing officials should cast off the limitations imposed by the Constitution. AMERICA'S FOUNDERS IMPOSED THOSE RESTRICTIONS TO PREVENT TYRANNY!

The government is trashing the foundational law of the land and telling us, *We don't need that old law. We know what justice is. You can trust us!* Such reasoning paves the way for tyrants! And every tyrant is a tool of the devil.

THE SECOND AMENDMENT

The lawless mindset of radical Democrats is exposed by their stance on gun control. They hate the Second Amendment and want to destroy the Constitution. Every time there is a mass shooting, even before any facts about the situation come out, they immediately begin pushing for gun bans. Many of them don't just want to raise the buying age or to restrict the sale of a few types of guns; they want to enact these measures on their way to confiscating all privately owned guns. *That will leave them with all the firepower.*

This attack on citizens' rights and the rule of law is chopping at the pillars of our nation.

On December 14, 2012, a young man named Adam Lanza killed twenty 6-to-7-year-old children in Newtown, Connecticut. He had some serious mental problems; he almost looked like a young girl; his parents were divorced; he was living with his mom, and his father wasn't around. Nearly every time a tragedy like this happens, there is a dysfunctional family in the background. Sin in our families can have catastrophic results.

Yet what is the solution, according to the radical-left politicians and the media? BAN THE GUNS.

On January 16, 2013, President Obama signed 23 executive actions on gun control. When he signed those orders, he surrounded himself with little children who had written letters to him asking, *Mr. President, would you please do something about the violence in schools?* Who wants to debate with him when he has children all around him?

In November 2015, after football player Jovan Belcher killed his girlfriend and then himself, Bob Costas said on an NFL broadcast on NBC that this wouldn't have happened if Belcher hadn't had a gun. A linebacker is big enough that he could have killed her without a weapon. But they're going after guns.

I'm told that NBC has some of the bloodiest movies on television. Yet it is telling Americans to get rid of the guns. Why don't we start with getting rid of the *bloody television programs?* Is it possible that is a bigger problem?

Mr. Obama and the left are so eager to ban guns. But what are they doing to stop drug cartels making inroads into America? In the Fast and Furious scandal, Attorney General Eric Holder gave heavy weapons to cartels and lost track of them. What about stopping the drug wars between gangs in America's big cities? What success did Mr. Obama ever have in preventing Chicago, his hometown, from becoming the murder capital of the nation?

The radical left wants to take the guns of law-abiding people. They know the criminals are not about to give up their guns.

The Second Amendment in the U.S. protects the people's right to bear arms, but for what? Leftists act as if its purpose is so Americans can go out and shoot deer.

That isn't the reason for the Second Amendment at all. THE MAIN POINT WAS TO PROTECT THE CITIZENS FROM GOVERNMENT TYRANNY. The government might decide to take over, and if you don't have guns or something to defend yourself, what are you going to do (unless you have God's protection)?

Why won't the radical liberals admit this? That is the real world our Founding Fathers came out of! That is the real world today. But the liberals dismiss and ridicule even the *thought* of government overreach. *Oh, please!* they say. *That could never happen!*

Can't we see the danger in a government, unconstrained by the law, disarming its citizens while heavily arming itself with military weapons, spy equipment and even drones that it feels justified in using at will?

GOVERNMENT TYRANNY IS ROUTINE IN HUMAN HISTORY, AND THEY KNOW IT. Why are they so deceitful? Is it because they have an ulterior motive? Let's not be naive and think something like that could never happen here. Our forefathers weren't stupid. They wanted to guarantee Americans' freedom. They knew that God is a God of freedom; He wants us to be free. That is a gift from God, and they understood that!

Do you remember how we gained our freedoms? A lot of people bled and a lot of people died to give us the freedoms we have today. If they hadn't armed themselves, faced death and even died for Americans, this country would be like most others in history: oppressed by tyrants.

"Jews are prohibited from acquiring, possessing and carrying firearms and ammunition, as well as truncheons or stabbing weapons. Those now possessing weapons and ammunition are at once to turn them over to the local police authority. Whoever willfully or negligently violates the provisions will be punished with imprisonment and a fine."

This is an executive order from 1938, just before World War II, signed by Adolf Hitler. He disarmed the Jews as a precursor to controlling them, herding them up, and eliminating them.

Mass shootings are *sickening.* But what makes me sicker is somebody using such massacres to promote a tyrannical political ideology! I am sickened by executive orders that circumvent the Constitution and by a president casting aside the law and doing whatever he wills! I am aghast at an American president acting like Antiochus did.

IGNORING THE CONSTITUTION

Throughout Obama's presidency, his government grew increasingly brazen about casting aside restraint and forcing its will on the public.

In 2010, the president signed his health-care plan into law even though most of the people said they didn't want it, not one Republican voted for it, and the Supreme Court was one vote away from striking it down. Though the administration had promised to always be transparent, it made all its decisions behind closed doors and assured us, *Don't worry, we'll take care of it. We know what's good for you.* But they DO NOT know what's good for us. That bill created many more problems than it supposedly solved. But these leaders never admit mistakes. They never apologize. And they *never* give back power once they have taken it.

In 2011, President Obama illegally launched a military offensive in Libya without consulting Congress. One representative said by unilaterally wielding the nation's military sword, the president had effectively "neutered" the legislature; another called it "an affront to our Constitution." Afterward, Libya aligned more closely with Iran, the world's top state sponsor of terrorism. Did that executive decision have a good outcome?

President Obama directed federal agencies to stop enforcing certain immigration laws. In 2014, he signed a raft of executive actions on immigration without going through Congress, actions that granted some form of amnesty to nearly 5 million illegal immigrants. Courts later ruled that this was unconstitutional. Yet these decisions undermined the meaning of American citizenship and permanently changed the nation's demographics. Of course, leftists stigmatize anyone as racist who doesn't celebrate this.

These are just a few of the many times Barack Obama broke the rules, overstepped his office, evaded constitutional checks on his power, and eroded the rule of law. They remind me of the old fable about the frog in the pot: Turn on the stove and heat the water slow enough, and before it realizes what is happening, the frog has boiled to death.

Barack Obama encouraged a *culture* of lawlessness within the government. Many officials grew more and more bold in doing what they felt was right regardless of, even in defiance of, the law.

It is not difficult to look back on these incidents as progressive steps that led to the eruption of lawlessness that undermined and overturned the 2020 presidential election.

Cass Sunstein was the head of the Office of Information Regulatory Affairs during Obama's first term, a position with a lot of power. In one of his books, Sunstein actually wrote that America would be far better off if it replaced democracy with technocracy—rule by an elite group of well-educated technocrats. The issues are too complicated for most people to understand, he said. One congressman said of Sunstein's view, "That belief is spread across the administration."

What kind of a government is that? America's founders dispersed power among the branches and made leaders accountable to the people. Would you like our country to be run by a few powerful, unaccountable technocrats who think like Sunstein and the radicals around Obama? That is precisely the form of government JOSEPH STALIN used! He PURGED AND MURDERED some 30 MILLION of his own people! He made Hitler look *tame* by comparison. That is what can happen with such a government.

Of course, these officials insist they can be trusted with such power. The truth is, we should have *zero* trust in the devil—and that is what this is truly about.

MILITARY UNDER ATTACK

The way President Obama undermined the rule of law, and even policing and law enforcement, exposed his lawless aims. This ambition had a dangerous corollary in another diabolical act—one that received almost no attention: As president, OBAMA GUTTED AMERICA'S MILITARY LEADERSHIP.

During his first five years in office, President Obama forced close to 200 generals and many other high-ranking officers out of their commands. He simply dismantled and replaced the leadership of our armed forces. Why?

Several retired generals certainly knew what was going on. Presidents often change some top military staff, but these men called what Obama did a "PURGE." Retired Army Maj. Gen. Patrick Brady said, "There is no doubt he is intent on EMASCULATING THE MILITARY." Retired Navy Capt. Joseph John said, "[T]he U.S. Armed Forces have been under RELENTLESS ATTACK by the occupant of the Oval Office for five years" (*World Net Daily*, Nov. 4, 2013). Retired Army Maj. Gen. Paul Vallely told *Investor's Business Daily* that Obama was "intentionally weakening and gutting our military, Pentagon and REDUCING US AS A SUPERPOWER, and anyone in the ranks who disagrees or speaks out is being purged" (Oct. 29, 2013). Yes, that was exactly his goal!

President Obama enfeebled America's armed forces in many ways: slashing the defense budget, reducing global deployments, prioritizing identity politics and diversity quotas over war-making capability. But *the liquidation of leaders was perhaps the deadliest.*

NO MATTER HOW POWERFUL, NUMEROUS OR SOPHISTICATED THE MILITARY, IF IT LACKS STRONG LEADERSHIP IT CAN ACCOMPLISH NOTHING.

The people Obama elevated to these commands prioritized political correctness, racial and gender crusading, and other outrageous causes that eviscerated America's defenses. They supported Obama allowing transgenders into the military. They directed resources toward promoting radical-leftist ideas in foreign countries rather than protecting America's interests and securing the globe.

Their goal was never to train soldiers to love their country and fight and even die to save their country. Often, these leaders trained soldiers to *hate* their own country!

These moves did not aim simply to "fundamentally *transform* America," but to fundamentally DESTROY America.

When Donald Trump became president, he worked to restore America's military might. But even he was disappointed with the poor quality of many of the leaders under his command.

Once Joe Biden assumed the presidency, he immediately resumed the Obama-era madness. He commanded officers to focus on expunging "racism" and "right-wing extremism" from the ranks. His administration offered "free gender-reassignment surgery," as if that would make them better soldiers. Reading lists for sailors and soldiers feature books that indoctrinate them in anti-American thinking. In 2021, when one lieutenant colonel wrote a book revealing how Marxism had infected the military elite, he was immediately fired. Prior generations of soldiers *sacrificed their lives* to defeat the ideology that this generation of soldiers is being taught in our military academies!

THESE DECISIONS BY AMERICA'S LEADERS HAVE DEADLY CONSEQUENCES. What happens when military commanders are more dedicated to promoting radical ideas than to defending the country? What happens when they don't even believe in the ideals of the nation they represent?

This dramatically fulfills the prophecy in Isaiah 3:1-3, where God promises to curse America by removing "[t]he mighty man, and the man of war, the judge, and the prophet, and the prudent, and the ancient, The captain of fifty, and the honourable man," and other effective leaders. Where are you headed when you are bereft of strong, honorable, law-abiding leadership?

SCANDAL AFTER SCANDAL

In one of his last official acts as president, Obama granted clemency to Oscar López Rivera, who belonged to a Marxist terrorist organization. The editor of the *Federalist*, Ben Domenech, wrote on Substack that López "recruited and trained a small army of terrorists to murder his fellow Americans. He built bomb factories. He taught the young and impressionable how to make devices that would kill and maim .... When he was put on trial, he admitted to doing all he had been accused of—he showed no remorse." Yet Obama granted him clemency.

This typifies the work of Antiochus. It is lawless. It unleashes forces of hatred and violence. It casts down truth to the ground. And it masquerades as mercy and kindness.

Having such a man at the helm in America has produced *bitter affliction.* The scandalous acts he and his administration perpetrated are too voluminous to count. Here, though, is a short list:

- Refusing to disclose foreign donors to his campaign
- Suddenly reversing his stance on homosexual "marriage"
- Refusing to enforce or actively trying to stop duly enacted laws on marriage and immigration
- Doubling the deficit
- Nearly doubling the national debt accumulated by the 43 preceding presidents combined
- Eroding average Americans' wealth
- Massively expanding food stamps and welfare
- Administration staff and agencies using secret e-mail accounts
- Funneling millions in government contracts to cronies
- The Department of Justice organizing racial protests
- Pushing sexual perversion on other countries through the State Department
- Spying on journalists, members of Congress and everyday Americans en masse
- White House staff involved in a prostitution scandal in Colombia
- Interfering in the FBI probe into Hillary Clinton's e-mails
- The Veterans Affairs scandal and cover-up
- The Environmental Protection Agency, Social Security Administration and other federal agencies buying large amounts of weapons and ammunition
- Praising the Chinese Communist system
- The corrupt auto industry bailout
- Denying 77 percent of Freedom of Information Act requests
- Spending $36 million in lawsuits to keep information secret
- Pushing public accommodation of transgenders
- Massive land seizures
- Spying on former Israeli Prime Minister Benjamin Netanyahu
- Pressuring Israel not to strike Iran's nuclear program

- Signing the New START Treaty that empowered Russia and weakened the U.S. (which Russia then violated, with no apparent consequences)
- Pulling out of Iraq and paving the way for the Islamic State terror regime
- Stopping an investigation into the Clinton Foundation
- Giving financial waivers to White House staff and allies
- Requiring religious groups to pay for abortion drugs
- Solyndra and other stimulus-receiving failures
- Suing states and other jurisdictions for enforcing the law
- Interfering with and possibly hacking certain elections
- Releasing five Guantanamo Bay terrorists in exchange for Islamist Bowe Bergdahl
- The Justice Department refusing court orders
- The State Department supporting a boycott of Israeli goods
- Funding a political campaign against Netanyahu
- Helping to draft a United Nations resolution against Israeli settlements
- Betraying Israel on the UN Security Council

Americans should have been sounding the alarm about these events with all their strength! Why weren't the media, even "conservative" media, *exposing* Obama's lawless, destructive actions? Some simply lacked the courage to stand up for our constitutional republic. Many others are themselves corrupt and have come to accept and support the president's toxic anti-Americanism.

For whatever reason, *nobody stood up against Barack Obama.*

COMMUNIST INFILTRATION

In 1956, Herbert W. Armstrong encapsulated the emerging threat of communism in America as "a psychological warfare of propaganda, infiltration, subversion, demoralization. It is a warfare that has attacked our minds and our moral and spiritual values, rather than our bodies and our earthly possessions."

Mr. Armstrong said that this warfare is actually described in biblical prophecies. "It's a kind of warfare we don't understand or know how to cope with," he wrote. "It uses every diabolical means to *weaken us from within,* sapping our strength, perverting our morals, sabotaging our educational system, wrecking our social structure, destroying our spiritual and religious life, weakening our industrial and economic power, demoralizing our armed forces, and finally, after such infiltration, overthrowing our government by force and violence!"

Think seriously about that statement. Look at America today. Have those Communist objectives been achieved? Morally and spiritually, the nation is filthy. We lead the world in pornography. We promote same-sex "marriage" and transgenderism and push other nations to embrace it. God says we have forgotten how to blush! (Jeremiah 6:15; 8:12). Religion, where it is practiced, is about feel-good self-help rather than obeying God and living by the Bible (Matthew 4:4). Our educational system produces millions of students who hate America, love communism and know nothing. Millions of Americans depend on handouts that enslave them to the government and to their human nature. The national debt has sailed past *$30 trillion.* Our military is powerful, but it is wielded by weak, "woke" leaders. Even among everyday Americans, our pride in our power is broken (Leviticus 26:19).

The Communist infiltration Mr. Armstrong warned about has happened. I don't claim to know the degree to which the *Communists* organized it, or that Mr. Obama fulfills a Communist plan (though there is some evidence to suggest that).

But I DO KNOW ABOUT THE DEVIL! And I know he is doing EVERYTHING HE CAN TO SINK AMERICA.

I have personally seen him use a man at the top, an Antiochus, to bring down God's Church. And I have watched as America's government, ruled by a man with a stated goal to fundamentally transform the nation, took one step after another to weaken this country, hastening the fulfillment of some of the most terrifying prophecies in the Bible! And I KNOW that the devil, who is a liar and who hates law, IS BEHIND THAT.

The fact that Americans have been casting the Constitution to the ground and encouraging lawlessness in their marriages, in their government and in their policy toward other nations has a definite CAUSE. The worst of it traces back to the fact that *Satan and millions of demons have been cast down* and confined to Earth (Revelation 12:9; see Appendix B). That is making an astounding, dumbfounding difference in what is happening around us.

Many people scoff about there even *being* a devil—while he is tearing them apart! They do not know God nor do they understand anything about Satan. Until they do, the problems will only intensify.

'BY REASON OF TRANSGRESSION'

The obvious question arises, why did God allow such a terrible thing to happen to America? The answer is in Daniel 8:10-12.

As I explained, these verses describe a Satan-led army of demons wreaking destruction within God's Church. And notice: It says it was *"by reason of transgression."* In other words, the *sins of the people* gave Satan his opening. Then he went right into the sanctuary, working through the leaders at the top, and cast the truth to the ground. That is how Satan destroyed God's Church. I watched it happen before my eyes.

Such devastation cannot be done from among the people. It can only be done from the top.

Now Satan and his mighty army of demons are destroying the superpower of end-time Israel the same way. THE VALUES THAT HELPED MAKE AMERICA GREAT ARE BEING CAST TO THE GROUND—FROM THE TOP.

And why? This is the part that many people overlook or reject: It is "by reason of transgression": because there is so much sin *within the people.* This is not merely a problem of one man at the top with a lawless spirit. He would never have achieved the heights of power if not for a massive crisis of lawbreaking throughout the nation! Our people are *saturated* in sin of every imaginable type—and proud of it!

There are consequences for such lawlessness. This is a clear principle spelled out in the Bible from beginning to end. *This* is why God punishes us with such a devastating curse. Many people pray for God to protect us from this satanic attack. But those prayers are not being answered—because of our sins.

Isaiah prophesied about our people today: "Ah SINFUL NATION, a people *laden with iniquity*, a seed of evildoers, children that are corrupters: they have forsaken the LORD, they have provoked the Holy One of Israel unto anger, they are gone away backward" (Isaiah 1:4).

This nation has had so many blessings for so many years. But this is rapidly changing, and God is warning us that it is about to get unimaginably worse!

Notice the prophecy in verse 7: "Your country is desolate, your cities are burned with fire: your land, strangers devour it in your presence, and it is desolate, as overthrown by strangers." This is speaking of massive *race wars* swallowing up our cities! AMERICA'S CITIES ARE GOING TO BURN.

This will be the end result of this attack on law. Do not be ignorant of Satan's devices. You can see his fingerprints all over what is happening today.

The *solution* to these problems is to reject satanic lawlessness. It is to *exalt truth* and refuse to allow it to be cast down to the ground.

Even respecting and enforcing the Constitution and the laws of the land would halt the decline and eliminate many of America's woes. But real, lasting recovery and progress will come only by repentance toward God (Ezekiel 33:11). We must return to honoring and obeying the *law of God.*

WORSHIPING THE WILL

W ORLD WAR II KILLED AN UNIMAGINABLE 60 MILLION PEOPLE and inflicted some of the worst suffering in history. And it was started by Adolf Hitler.

Hitler believed that if you tell a big lie and repeat it often enough, people will believe it. He wrote in *Mein Kampf*, "[I]n *the big lie* there is always a certain force of credibility; because the broad masses of a nation are always more easily corrupted in the deeper strata of their emotional nature than consciously or voluntarily; and thus in the primitive simplicity of their minds *they more readily fall victims to the big lie than the small lie*, since they themselves often tell small lies in little matters but would be ashamed to resort to large-scale falsehoods."

That may sound strange, but Hitler used it with frightening effectiveness. He claimed that the German Army did not lose World War I on the battlefield, but instead had been stabbed in the back by the Jews. There was no evidence for this claim, but Hitler repeated it until people fell for it. He blamed the Versailles Treaty and held the West responsible for the political and economic turmoil plaguing Germany's Weimar Republic. Germans came to believe Hitler, elected him chancellor, and supported his industrial-scale extermination of some 6 million Jews.

We have not learned from this history as we should. Could something similar happen today? Could someone stir up a political revolution simply by repeating a blatant lie over and over and over until enough people believe it?

Could it happen in America? Well, it ABSOLUTELY HAS ALREADY HAPPENED to a shocking degree!

Hermann Rauschning was president of the Free City of Danzig in Germany from 1933 to 1934. He briefly joined the Nazi movement before breaking with it. He had many conversations with Hitler that he later wrote down in his book *Hitler Speaks.*

He wrote that during these talks, Hitler spoke a lot about the *psychology of lying.* Rauschning recalled that on one occasion, Hitler said: "What you tell people in the mass in a receptive state of fanatic devotion will remain. Words received under a hypnotic influence are *radical* and *impervious to every reasonable explanation."* He also recalled Hitler on other occasions saying: "We are now at the end of the Age of Reason"; "A new age of *magic interpretation* of the world is coming, of interpretation in terms of the will and not of intelligence"; "There is no such thing as truth either in the moral or the scientific sense."

You must come to recognize how THIS SAME SPIRIT SATURATES THE RADICAL LEFT IN AMERICAN POLITICS.

From where did Hitler get that *psychology of lying?* The answer is in John 8:44, where Jesus Christ said of Satan the devil that he "abode not in the truth, because there is no truth in him. When he speaketh a lie, he speaketh of his own: for *he is a liar, and the father of it."*

Rauschning called Hitler a "master enchanter." Hitler had an intense fascination with occult magic. Much of what he told Rauschning about *"a new age of magic interpretation"* came from the German occultist Ernst Schertel. Schertel's *Magic: History, Theory and Practice* was one of the most heavily annotated books in Hitler's personal library.

Hitler's annotations include highlights such as "the difference between 'true' and 'false' has disappeared," and "quite a lot is gained with [magic]: namely the possibility to ... CHANGE THE WORLD ACCORDING TO OUR WILL. But this is magic, and on this basis we are able to create reality where no reality is."

Hitler believed he did not need to rely on reason, intelligence, reality, truth or God. Instead, he worshiped his own human will and believed he could *create his own reality.*

Consciously or subconsciously, a great many people today believe the same thing. They just lie until they convince not only those around them but even themselves that they are right!

We are seeing bold, blatant lies become a bigger and bigger part of today's political landscape. It is stunning how utterly unapologetic our leaders have become in saying things that are clearly, provably false. And in the rare cases when they are caught and called out, they say they never said those things, or they insist that what is false is actually true. They are SHAMELESS!

Isn't this exactly what Hitler was describing? These people believe that if they *say* something, it is true! They think that if they WILL it, then everyone should believe them.

This is a sure sign of Satan's growing power. We are seeing the work of this lying murderer at his worst! He is the father of lies; there is no truth in him. But he will still look you boldly in the eye and insist that everything he says is the truth!

When campaigning for a second term, Obama said, "You may be frustrated sometimes with the pace of change. I'm frustrated too sometimes. But you know where I stand. You know what I believe. YOU KNOW I TELL THE TRUTH." That was a mountainous lie!

Conservative commentator Glenn Beck responded to the president's statement: "This is more a judgment on America and the press. I've never looked back and marveled at how many people will fall for and accept, knowingly accept, a falsehood. I'VE NEVER SEEN IT BEFORE IN MY LIFE."

THAT IS BECAUSE TIMES ARE DIFFERENT! You can't explain this kind of unprecedentedly open, brazen deceit unless you go to the Bible and realize that Satan has been cast down and that his influence is greater than ever!

This is a terribly dangerous trend: people *using lies* to achieve political ambitions, to impose a radical agenda on others, and to destroy people's lives.

Barack Obama is followed by people in government and in the media who *worship the will,* and he dominates. Those people are following that will! And in truth, Obama is actually following that will, too. He and the others do not realize that *they are following Satan's will!*

MASS FORMATION PSYCHOSIS

One unmistakable example of this phenomenon is the way American politicians responded to COVID-19. They exaggerated the threat of the virus, assumed unprecedented powers, and used those to take radical measures that destroyed hundreds of thousands of businesses, locked people up within their own homes, disrupted the education of millions of children, turned people against each other by encouraging them to report their neighbors—they perpetrated untold problems. Then they promoted experimental vaccines, even mandating them for people to keep their jobs or use basic services. They trampled the Bill of Rights. They censored truth and told lie upon lie.

Yet millions of people went right along with them!

Dr. Robert Malone, who helped make the major breakthrough in mRNA study in 1988 that laid the foundation for the mRNA technology used in millions of COVID-19 vaccine shots, compared society's response today to what happened in Germany during the 1920s and '30s. There you had a "very intelligent, highly educated population, and they went barking mad. And how did that happen? The answer is mass formation psychosis," he told Joe Rogan on January 3, 2022.

"When you have a society that has become decoupled from each other and has free-floating anxiety and a sense that 'things don't make sense, we can't understand it'—and then their attention gets focused by a leader or series of events on one small point—just like hypnosis, they literally become hypnotized, and can be led anywhere," he said. Dr. Malone said an unscrupulous leader can take advantage of that to get his people to do *anything.*

"It doesn't matter whether they lied to them, or whatever. The data are irrelevant," he continued. "And furthermore, anybody who questions that narrative is to be immediately attacked. They are the 'other.' This is central to mass formation psychosis. And this is what has happened."

There is a definite reason why masses of people have done and are doing insane things. It stems from people trusting their own will—relying on and exalting their emotions, urges and even reasonings—rather than submitting to God's will.

The Apostle Paul wrote about this subject: "Let no man beguile you of your reward in a voluntary humility and worshipping of angels [*demons*, it should read], intruding into those things which he [*has*] seen [that is the correct translation], vainly puffed up by his fleshly mind .... Which things have indeed a shew of wisdom in WILL WORSHIP ..." (Colossians 2:18, 23).

This is exactly what Hitler was talking about: *will worship.* He spoke of "magic interpretation ... in terms of the will." Hitler said, in effect, *This is how it works now: Your logic, facts, evidence and truth won't stop us. We follow a "magic interpretation" today.* Will worship is impervious to truth. It insists that there *is* no absolute truth. *Don't look to the Bible for answers; you can have a magic interpretation of things.* The implication is, *Just follow* OUR *will!*

Paul reveals what happens when you worship the human will: It leads to worshiping *demons!* That is because the human mind is so vulnerable to the broadcasting, deception and influence of the "prince of the power of the air, the spirit that now worketh in the children of disobedience," Satan the devil (Ephesians 2:2). This is especially true of a mind full of vanity, like Satan's is.

Following a *human will* really means following *Satan's will!*

When human beings reject God's truth, they start worshiping their own opinions. They start thinking like Satan. When this type of thinking becomes entrenched enough, *people stop even caring about the difference between true and false.* THEY START TRYING TO MAGICALLY "CREATE REALITY WHERE NO REALITY IS." Satan's broadcasts make us *impervious to reason*—if we allow it.

That is the new age Hitler worked toward. That is the world Satan wants.

THIS INFLUENCE HAS TAKEN OVER AMERICA'S POLITICAL SCENE. Can you recognize it?

Paul warned not to let anyone beguile you this way: "Beware lest any man spoil you through philosophy and vain deceit, after the tradition of men, after the rudiments of the world, and not after Christ" (Colossians 2:8). The *Good News Bible* translates the expression "rudiments of the world" as "RULING SPIRITS OF THE UNIVERSE." *Thayer's Lexicon* says it means "to invade, of evils coming into existence among men and beginning to exert their power ...."

What is will worship? It means being ruled by THE DEMON WORLD! That is what Paul warned against in Colossians 2.

There is an evil spirit world. There are spirit beings, and they have real *power!* You cannot explain what happened to the Germans in the 1930s or the Americans in the 2020s or other such episodes in history any other way.

Scripture makes this reality exceedingly plain. Read the Gospels, for example, and you see that Jesus Christ frequently cast out demons. Where did those demons go? They didn't die. Millions of them are cast down and CONFINED TO THIS EARTH ALONG WITH SATAN THE DEVIL (Revelation 12:7-12).

If you are not rooted in God's Word, you are, as Hitler said, "easily corrupted in the deeper strata of [your] emotional nature."

Bible prophecy shows that *will worship* is going to lead to fierce, intense suffering—even worse than it did in World War II. The only way to escape the devastating catastrophes prophesied to engulf America is to be rooted in TRUTH—based on the *Word of God.*

CHAPTER THREE

SAVING AMERICA– TEMPORARILY

THE DESTRUCTIVE TRENDS OF THE OBAMA YEARS WERE FAR more dangerous than most people realized at the time. People were naive and ignorant about the extent of the threat. Even most Republican leaders failed to realize what they were dealing with: *people committed to destroying the government of this land.* We were witnessing a government—and a nation—on the verge of collapse!

Then something abruptly changed. In a result that shocked the radical leftists and surprised most of the nation, Donald J. Trump won the 2016 United States presidential election.

Mr. Trump's bid for the presidency was derided and mocked. The media called it a joke and clown show. Polls showed him considerably behind his opponent, Hillary Clinton, even just before the election. Yet somehow, what many dismissed as impossible happened. I will show you that his victory was miraculous intervention from God.

Once Donald Trump became president, something else extraordinary happened. His presidency temporarily STOPPED the forces destroying the country.

Mrs. Clinton's stated goal was to continue the legacy of Barack Obama. If she had become president, the ruinous trends of the Obama presidency would have continued and intensified. Many people—including me—believe it would have meant an end to our constitutional republic!

I want to show you that Mr. Trump's presidency was actually

prophesied in your Bible. It was *only* his election that prevented even worse troubles from bringing this nation down even more quickly—and God was behind it!

I will show you something else you may find stunning: God prophesies that Mr. Trump will return to power. Prophecy tells us what *God* thinks of the Biden presidency. But it also shows that what Trump accomplishes upon his return will prove to be only a temporary deliverance for the nation.

FORMER PROPHETS

Few people regard Bible prophecy as reliable. But you simply cannot understand events in America today without it.

The Old Testament is divided into three main sections: the law, the prophets and the writings. The prophets section includes the major and minor prophets, as well as the *former prophets,* which include the biblical books of Joshua, Judges, 1 and 2 Samuel, and 1 and 2 Kings. These books record a broad sweep of history of the nation of Israel—from the time the Israelites entered the Promised Land, through the division of the nation into the kingdoms of Israel and Judah, until both kingdoms were conquered and enslaved.

Americans today, and all people, can learn the real causes of world events by studying biblical prophecy, including the former prophets. There is a special message in all these books. The former prophets are mostly about history, but they are called former PROPHETS for good reason. THESE BOOKS WERE WRITTEN BY PROPHETS, and THEY ARE FILLED WITH END-TIME PROPHECY.

Many people believe the former prophets contain only history. That is not true, but even if it were, it would make these biblical books extremely valuable. Many authorities call history our most effective teacher. There is a lot of truth to that statement. And Bible history is the greatest of all because it is God's history.

There is a crucial reason why, of all the mountains of human history God could have miraculously recorded and preserved,

He chose *this* history. The principles illustrated here apply to all human beings. But also, because Americans are direct descendants of the Israelites (as proved in *The United States and Britain in Prophecy*), this history is specific PROPHECY FOR THEM.

Most of the history recorded in these books is prophetic. Perhaps the main example is how the state of religion in ancient Israel determined the state of the nation. This history indirectly prophesies what will happen to the modern descendants of Israel and Judah if we have similar religious problems. It shows that if we live the same lifestyles our forefathers did, we will experience the same results, good or bad. In this way, history prophesies the fate of nations—whether they will thrive or collapse!

But the former prophets are even more. These books contain many *direct* prophecies from God. They contain pivotal prophecies MAINLY FOR THE LATTER DAYS, OUR GENERATION TODAY. These books contain repeated references to the prophesied return of Jesus Christ, for example. They also contain other direct prophecies that, like much of the Bible, follow the principle of *duality:* There is an ancient fulfillment and a latter-day fulfillment, a type and an antitype.*

This invaluable material in the former prophets is available for us to study and learn from. We ought to be intensely interested in these biblical books.

There is an event in the history of ancient Israel that closely parallels what has happened in America.

KING JEROBOAM II

After the reigns of King David and King Solomon, 10 of the 12 tribes of Israel broke away from Judah and formed a separate nation, the kingdom of Israel. Their rebellion against the throne of David, inspired by their first king, Jeroboam I, proved to be a catastrophic mistake. Israel never had a righteous king again,

---

* To learn more, see Appendix A: "Prophetic Duality."

and as a result, it suffered continual curses and, some 200 years later, conquest and captivity.

This history is recorded in 2 Kings. Notice what 2 Kings 14 records about one of Israel's *last kings* before its fall: "In the fifteenth year of Amaziah the son of Joash king of Judah JEROBOAM the son of Joash king of Israel began to reign in Samaria, and reigned forty and one years. And he did that which was evil in the sight of the LORD: he departed not from all the sins of Jeroboam the son of Nebat, who made Israel to sin" (verses 23-24).

King Jeroboam II was *not* a righteous man. He did evil and committed the same sins that the first Jeroboam had. Nevertheless, the Bible records something remarkable: *God actually used this unrighteous king to help the nation.*

Notice this carefully: Jeroboam II "restored the coast of Israel from the entering of Hamath unto the sea of the plain, according to the word of the LORD God of Israel, which he spake by the hand of his servant Jonah ..." (verse 25). Jonah is well known for his warning to Nineveh. But before that, Jonah prophesied that Israel would expand its power, regain cities that had been lost to Syria, and prosper. This prophecy was fulfilled under Jeroboam II: Israel became more powerful than at any time since the days of Solomon!

Israel was still in a sinful state. Jeroboam II followed in the same rebellious traditions of the original Jeroboam. It wasn't because of the repentance or righteousness of the Israelites and their king that the nation experienced this resurgence. Why, then, did God bless the nation like it hadn't been blessed in two centuries?

"FOR THE LORD SAW THE AFFLICTION OF ISRAEL, THAT IT WAS VERY BITTER: FOR THERE WAS NOT ANY SHUT UP, NOR ANY LEFT, NOR ANY HELPER FOR ISRAEL" (verse 26). The Ferrar Fenton translation reads, "For the Ever-living pitied the immeasurable miseries of Israel both without and within, when there was no ease for Israel."

The Bible shows that anciently, God raised up the kingdom of Israel to represent Him. Satan attacked that nation in every way he could. History shows that at one point in the ninth century B.C., an enemy almost completely *destroyed* it—but God intervened.

How? He raised up a human king to temporarily save the nation. Notice verse 27: "And the LORD said not that he would blot out the name of Israel from under heaven: but HE SAVED THEM BY THE HAND OF JEROBOAM THE SON OF JOASH."

Israel was in *bitter affliction*—on the verge of being blotted out of existence! There was an effort to BLOT OUT THE NAME OF ISRAEL—a very satanic goal.

In God's plan, physical Israel was merely the *forerunner* of God's SPIRITUAL nation—His Church—to whom He *would* give His Holy Spirit and offer spiritual salvation. "[T]he Old Covenant with Israel at Sinai was a type and forerunner of the NEW COVENANT. It will be made with the New Testament CHURCH, which is the *spiritual* Israel and Judah (Jeremiah 31:31; Hebrews 8:6, 10)," Herbert W. Armstrong explained in his book *Mystery of the Ages.*

God's New Testament Church is ISRAEL, spiritually. Ephesians 2:11-19 show that, upon repentance, belief and conversion, *anyone* of *any nation or race* becomes part of spiritual Israel.

Spiritual Israel is meant to help lead the *entire world* to God. And God's ultimate purpose is to offer *all people who have ever lived* the opportunity to be a part of His eternal spiritual Family.

"Consider WHY God created mankind in the first place!" Mr. Armstrong wrote. "GOD IS REPRODUCING HIMSELF THROUGH MAN! He is creating in MAN God's own perfect holy and righteous spiritual CHARACTER! And that, in turn, is purposed to *restore* the GOVERNMENT OF GOD over all the Earth. And, further, to create BILLIONS OF GOD BEINGS TO FINISH THE CREATION OF THE VAST UNFINISHED UNIVERSE!"

This is a spectacular spiritual prophecy that you can absolutely prove from your Bible. This is ultimately what the name "Israel" represents. (It is explained more thoroughly in my book *The Former Prophets.*)

So what is "the name of Israel from under heaven"? It is God's MASTER PLAN TO RE-CREATE HIMSELF IN MANKIND. This is about *all of mankind* "UNDER HEAVEN"! Every human being who has ever lived on Earth—*under heaven*—will get an opportunity to receive the name of *spiritual* Israel—just as you see in the Church of God today. God's true Church has members of all races. ALL people will be able to receive God's Holy Spirit and a chance to be born into God's Kingdom, or Family, forever.

THIS IS THE INCREDIBLE HOPE IN THE NAME OF ISRAEL "UNDER HEAVEN"! IT EXPANDS TO A MAJESTIC VISION THAT REACHES FAR BEYOND THIS EARTH! God begins our spiritual lives "under heaven"—but His plan is to take us ABOVE HEAVEN to rule the entire universe forever under His direction.

Think about that: This means that someone who rejects "the name of Israel" is rejecting God and His Bible!

Satan hates everything God is about and wants to destroy all He does. Throughout history, Satan has continually tried to "blot out the name of Israel," that of God's chosen nation. Several biblical examples show this, as do historical examples up to the present day. Psalm 83 even prophesies that the devil will inspire an alliance of nations in the end time to try to destroy Israel and wipe out all memory of its name!

During this period of Israel's history, had God not intervened, the devil's plan to blot out the name of Israel would have prevailed! But God granted mercy when Israel really didn't deserve it. Rather than sending Israel into captivity at that time, God used this king to save Israel and give the nation one last period of prosperity before facing a reckoning for the sins it never repented of.

God saved Israel—"by the hand of" King Jeroboam II.

Despite the curses Israel was under, and despite the sins of Jeroboam and the wickedness of the nation, Jeroboam reigned for 41 years. He was the longest-reigning king in the history of the northern kingdom. Most other kings died by intrigue or betrayal, but Jeroboam's reign did not suffer from such violence and curses. The nation experienced a period of relative strength, stability and even prosperity.

This resurgence was not because of any personal greatness or leadership skill by Jeroboam. It was because God took pity on Israel in its affliction. It was because God chose not to let the name of Israel be blotted out. It was because God saved Israel!

But that resurgence *was temporary.* Israel did not thank God for the blessings, nor repent before God. And soon after, Israel was conquered and its people were taken captive by the Assyrians.

This prophetic history is especially relevant today. Remember the prophetic principle of duality. *History is repeating itself.*

Prophetically, the name of Israel that is in danger of being blotted out rests on the modern nations descended from ancient Israel, especially America and Britain.

Our people don't understand their Bibles as they once did. They don't understand the many scriptures about Satan the devil. But these scriptures show that the devil has his agenda against America, and only God can protect us.

A MODERN JEROBOAM

"During the long and peaceful reign of Jeroboam ii … the house of Israel had been lulled into a false sense of security," a February 1978 *Plain Truth* article explained. "National borders had been extended to their maximum, and the country was basking in comparative opulence and prosperity. Religious activity and ceremony was at a peak, and the people had come to believe that God was benignly smiling down upon them.

"Into this scene of national self-satisfaction stepped the Prophet Amos." You can see Amos's indictment of materialistic, luxury-glutted Israel in passages like Amos 6:1-6. His message was unpopular and "met with immediate opposition from the religious and political elements of his nation. He was even accused of conspiracy and disloyalty to the royal house."

This confrontation between prophet and king is described in Amos 7. THESE ANCIENT EVENTS WERE ONLY A *TYPE* OF END-TIME EVENTS, AS IS SO OFTEN THE CASE WITH PROPHETIC DUALITY.

In the prophecy of 2 Kings 14, much of the suffering is inflicted from *within the nation.* The nation is being destroyed from the inside by Antiochus and his supporters! The name of Israel is about to be blotted out. Then GOD HIMSELF INTERVENES AND SAVES ISRAEL TEMPORARILY. HOW? BY THE HAND OF AN END-TIME JEROBOAM.

The U.S. is the most prominent and powerful of the nations descended from ancient Israel. Britain and the Jewish state of Israel (biblical and prophetic Judah) rely heavily on the American superpower. And this prophecy shows that the U.S. will be ruled by a modern-day "Jeroboam."

Who is Jeroboam? Who is this *specific man* that Amos prophesies will be ruling the superpower of Israel when God gives it His final prophetic warning? (See Amos 7:8-9.)

For eight years under President Obama, the forces of the radical left were on the march. Even Republican leaders caved in, and that was after they had taken control of Congress and had considerable power to stop the president!

Donald Trump proved willing to take a stand where others have not. It was quite something to behold him resisting these anti-American forces! He also inspired a few other leaders to challenge the radical leftists and help expose them for who they are.

When you compare what Donald Trump did to what his predecessor did, there was a striking change. His presidency slowed the speed and force by which America was being pulled apart. He did not trash the Constitution as the previous president did. He passed tax cuts that helped many American families. He rolled back the universal health-care mandate and removed regulations that oppressed American businesses. The stock market broke new records.

Out of His mercy, God wanted to prevent the destruction of the nation, and He used President Trump to do it. Not because of that man's righteousness, but because he has the courage to step out and fight and knows it is the right thing to do.

Mr. Trump also has a strong relationship with religious leaders and has strongly defended religious groups. He speaks publicly about how good and strong and even righteous America is—

although the truth is that America today is none of those things. He inspired confidence in a lot of people about this nation's future. This was all a modern-day fulfillment of what happened in ancient Israel under Jeroboam II: a bit of a resurgence, some renewed prosperity, a swell of religious activity—*but not the true religion of the Bible*—with the blessing of the "king." It was a time of many people being lulled into a false sense of security and a belief that God was with them. Meanwhile, the spiritual character of the leader was deeply flawed, and the sins of the people grew worse.

It is critical that we realize *why* God brought about an American resurgence under Donald Trump's presidency. God Himself was pushing back against the Satan-inspired forces that would have blotted out the name of Israel, including *spiritual* Israel, God's own Church. He exposed those forces so that we could see them clearly. Donald Trump is the modern King Jeroboam II.

ONE LAST OPPORTUNITY TO REPENT

Realize that these prophecies do not end with America remaining perpetually prosperous and peaceful. This resurgence is temporary, just as it was in Israel under Jeroboam II.

After Jeroboam's reign ended, the kingdom of Israel was destroyed by Assyria (2 Kings 18). Prophecies in Isaiah 10 and Habakkuk 1 tell us this will happen to prophetic Israel in the end time too: America, the British peoples and biblical Judah (called Israel today) will be destroyed by a European empire led by Germany—descendants of the ancient Assyrians. We will look more into those prophecies later in this book.

THE MODERN NATIONS OF ISRAEL HAVE FORSAKEN GOD. They know virtually nothing about the Bible and our adversary, the devil.

Prophecies in Amos 7 and 2 Kings 14 reveal *why* God is saving America through Jeroboam. America is the superpower of these three nations and their peoples. God is *not* going to allow Mr. Obama and the radical left to blot out the name of Israel. He will expose this conspiracy so the world can see the truth.

America's temporary resurgence gives these three nations and their peoples one last chance to repent, but that window will remain open only for a few short years or less! Soon we will face consequences for not heeding God's warning—as you will see in later chapters.

Jeroboam II was the last king of Israel to receive a direct warning from God's prophets. He rejected God's correction. After his reign, there were six more evil, mostly short-lived kings—men who came to power through murder or other ignoble means. They allied with Syria to fight off a rising threat from Assyria, the next dominant regional power (just as Amos had prophesied). In the end, they were forced to pay tribute to Assyria, then ultimately conquered and led away captive by the Assyrians.

A similar nightmarish fate awaits America! Over a hundred biblical prophecies warn of this same punishment for our sins.

God will make America great again! But the Bible shows that He will do so only *after* hard correction. God is giving these warnings in an effort to *save people* from that fate. He is extending mercy for a short while before the punishment is carried out. Use this opportunity to prove this truth, heed the warning, and accept God's offer of protection to you.

Speaking of this time, God says in Ezekiel 33:11, "I have no pleasure in the death of the wicked; but that the wicked turn from his way and live: TURN YE, TURN YE FROM YOUR EVIL WAYS; FOR WHY WILL YE DIE, O HOUSE OF ISRAEL?"

God is deeply emotional about this! When He saves Israel, it is only temporary. But He yearns to save Israel *permanently!* He derives no pleasure in seeing people suffer. This is why He pleads with these people, crying out through His faithful work, beseeching them to repent of their sins.

God is full of mercy and love, and He is quick to forgive and protect. But to receive God's forgiveness and protection, the people of America—and any person of any race or nation—must *repent.* We must stop sinning, stop rebelling against God's law, and stop resisting God.

CHAPTER FOUR

LIES AND TREASON

URING HIS EIGHT YEARS AS PRESIDENT, BARACK OBAMA and the radical left operated with stunning latitude and abandon in sabotaging America. As they prepared for the transition to Obama's successor, their determination to preserve their grip on power through a Hillary Clinton presidency propelled them to unparalleled evils.

When Donald Trump was a presidential candidate in 2016, radical leftists targeted him, ridiculed him for saying the election could be rigged, and did all they could, with the collusion of a biased media, to portray him as unfit for office. But they did much more. They committed serious crimes. The extent of their lawless activity took time to be uncovered, and surely some of it has yet to be fully exposed.

We now know that in 2016 the presidential campaign of Hillary Clinton and the Democratic National Committee paid law firm Perkins Coie for a report by Fusion GPS, a research firm based in Washington, D.C. Fusion GPS paid former British MI-6 intelligence agent Christopher Steele to compile smears and slanders against Clinton's political opponent. In September 2016, Steele confessed to a senior Justice Department official that he "was desperate that Donald Trump not get elected and was passionate about him not being president." *This* was the man Democrats hired to find condemning information about Mr. Trump. Would a biased source like him have any motivation to *lie?* This shows how obsessed they were with stopping Trump.

Steele created a 35-page dossier as opposition research for Hillary Clinton's campaign. Opposition research is often full of inaccuracies and, at times, outright lies. Steele's report falsely accused Donald Trump of disgusting escapades with Russian prostitutes, among other slanders, and said Russian President Vladimir Putin could use this secret information to blackmail Mr. Trump if he became president. It also alleged collusion between the Russian government and Donald Trump's presidential campaign. It was based on "bar talk" (according to one of his sources, who was a Russian citizen), unsolicited phone calls from anonymous sources, lies concocted by Fusion GPS, and illegally obtained Internet data.

Normally, "dirt" like what Steele compiled would never make it past media newsrooms. But this case was different. When Fusion GPS employees, along with Steele himself, farmed the dossier out to the media piecemeal, the press published it with relish. It wasn't until BuzzFeed published the entirety of Steele's report on January 11, 2017, that the public finally got a look at the only source for the rumors they had been fed over the past six months.

Even more diabolical, the federal government, without bothering to verify anything in the dossier, began using it as evidence to justify spying on Trump and members of his campaign.

In the fall of 2020, Director of National Intelligence John Ratcliffe declassified critical documents exposing the fact that the Steele dossier and the plot against Donald Trump traced all the way up to top officials in the Obama administration— INCLUDING PRESIDENT BARACK OBAMA HIMSELF.

This reveals an unprecedented level of corruption and lawlessness. It is a NATION-DESTROYING problem!

THE HIGHEST LEVELS OF GOVERNMENT

America's intelligence and law enforcement agencies—the Federal Bureau of Investigation, the Central Intelligence Agency, the National Security Agency and others—are supposed to be fair and politically neutral. But mountains of information have come out regarding events surrounding the 2016 election that expose shocking political bias within these federal entities. These officials routinely covered up egregious lawbreaking by Clinton and other Democrats and did everything possible to find or even create scandal associated with Mr. Trump.

Among the documents Ratcliffe released to the Senate Judiciary Committee was a redacted copy of CIA Director John Brennan's handwritten notes after briefing President Obama in July 2016 on recent intelligence the CIA had received. His notes read: "We're getting additional insight into Russian activities from [redacted]. Cite alleged approval by Hillary Clinton on 28 July of a proposal from one of her foreign-policy advisers to villify [sic] Donald Trump by stirring up a scandal claiming interference by the Russian security service."

These notes prove that Brennan and Obama knew all about the Steele dossier and what a fraud it was.

In his letter to the Senate Judiciary Committee, Ratcliffe wrote, "In late July 2016, U.S. intelligence agencies obtained insight into Russian intelligence analysis alleging that U.S. presidential candidate Hillary Clinton had approved a campaign plan to stir up a scandal against U.S. presidential candidate Donald Trump by tying him to Putin and the Russians' hacking of the Democratic National Committee [DNC]."

That was a reference to an event that summer, when the DNC said it had been hacked. Immediately the Clinton campaign said that the Russian government had perpetrated the hack and that its motive was to help Mr. Trump win the election. Julian Assange and WikiLeaks say that was a complete fabrication. The only people who were given access to analyze the DNC computer system and confirm what had happened were from CrowdStrike, a cybersecurity firm hired by the DNC, which was working against Donald Trump.

The DNC hack is what laid the foundation for the media, Democrats and Obama officials TO BEGIN BUILDING THEIR CONSPIRACY THEORY THAT DONALD TRUMP WAS COLLUDING

WITH VLADIMIR PUTIN.* THAT FRAUD WAS ALL THEY HAD! It was all intended to divert the focus from the content of the DNC e-mails—and to slander and destroy Mr. Trump.

President Obama was aware of this, too.

In early August 2016, three months before the election, James Clapper, director of the Office of National Intelligence, along with FBI Director James Comey and CIA Director Brennan, briefed President Obama and Vice President Joe Biden about the Steele dossier. It has since been proved that all these men knew the report was rubbish. Brennan's notes show that they knew it was a plan Hillary Clinton had concocted "to vilify Donald Trump" and to falsely accuse him of ties to Russia. THE WHOLE INTELLIGENCE COMMUNITY KNEW IT WAS A FRAUD. I believe that Obama knew about it before then, but it is *certain* he knew three months before the 2016 election.

Ratcliffe's letter continued: "On 7 September 2016, U.S. intelligence officials forwarded an investigative referral to FBI Director James Comey and Deputy Assistant Director of Counterintelligence Peter Strzok regarding 'U.S. presidential candidate Hillary Clinton's approval of a plan concerning U.S. presidential candidate Donald Trump and Russian hackers hampering U.S. elections as a means of distracting the public from her use of a private mail server.'"

Note that! The FBI received "an investigative referral" from U.S. intelligence officials. This means somebody in the Obama administration was *telling* the FBI to investigate these phony allegations against Trump. Obama and everyone in his circle, the intelligence agencies and the FBI, all knew that the idea of the Trump campaign colluding with the Russian government was created by Hillary Clinton's campaign and was a hoax. But they were willing to use it so they could carry on with their lawless rule over the country!

---

* CrowdStrike CEO Shawn Henry testified at a closed-door hearing on December 5, 2017, that the allegation that the DNC data was hacked by Russia is based on "circumstantial evidence."

Ratcliffe later said he has *over a thousand classified documents* relating to the Steele dossier and how it was used "at the highest levels of our government." He said the contents of those documents are criminal!

Eighteen days before the 2016 election, on October 21, the FBI and the Department of Justice presented this vile, deceitful dossier to the Foreign Intelligence Surveillance Act (FISA) court. Knowing it was garbage, Obama's enforcement agents used this report to obtain approval to electronically surveil Trump campaign staff member Carter Page. They had tried to get a FISA warrant on Page once before; it wasn't until they had the Steele dossier and media reports (sourced to Steele) that they were able to secure the warrant. This may seem insignificant, since Page was a lower-level, volunteer staff member in the Trump campaign. But such a warrant can be used to track all the target's communications, including any he may have had with then candidate Trump. *This secret warrant actually opened the door to spy on everyone surrounding Mr. Trump.* THAT WAS ITS PURPOSE.

THIS IS BLATANT CRIMINAL ACTIVITY AT THE HIGHEST LEVELS OF GOVERNMENT!

A December 2019 report from Department of Justice Inspector General Michael Horowitz included this statement: "We concluded that the Crossfire Hurricane team's receipt of Steele's election reporting on September 19, 2016, played a central and essential role" in obtaining the FISA warrant. FBI Associate Deputy Director Andrew McCabe also admitted that the FBI operations traced back to the Steele dossier. In fact, those law enforcement officials had to renew that warrant *three times* to keep spying. Each time, these agencies had to convince the FISA court that America faced a dangerous threat from abroad, such as a terrorist attack. They had no actual evidence, so they relied on the Steele dossier and concealed from the court the fact that it traced straight back to the Clinton campaign.

Steele admitted in a British court that he had leaked information from his dossier to the press in September

2016—a month before the FISA warrant based on his dossier was approved. He lied to the FBI that he was keeping the dossier confidential, showing himself to be an unreliable source. The FBI ended the relationship with him right after obtaining the warrant, but Steele's dossier continued to flow into the FBI through Bruce Ohr and his wife. The FBI continued to withhold evidence proving Carter Page's innocence from the FISA court and relied on Steele's report for three more warrant renewals.

Horowitz also reported that the FBI disseminated the Steele accusations to the intelligence agencies and sought to include them in the January 2017 Intelligence Community Assessment. The order to do that came from OBAMA HIMSELF!

This event alone shows that Barack Obama was in charge of the dossier and the intelligence community. He was orchestrating all the significant events. You will see that in this book.

The dossier was effectively an "insurance policy" intended to destroy Trump in the event—in their minds remote, even inconceivable—that Mrs. Clinton lost on November 8. Yet somehow, Donald Trump pulled off the impossible and won.

This shocked the radical Democrats. And suddenly, they faced the ghastly prospect of an incoming presidential administration that would discover and expose their rank lawlessness.

Barack Obama then ramped up his treasonous plot to cover up their prior actions at all costs—and worked to politically destroy the elected president of the United States.

A TREASONOUS MEETING

On January 5, 2017, President Obama met with his top intelligence officials in the Oval Office to get a briefing on the progress of the Russia-Trump investigation. This crucial meeting included Comey, Brennan, Clapper and Biden, as well as NSA Director Michael Rogers, National Security Adviser Susan Rice and Deputy Attorney General Sally Yates. VIRTUALLY

ALL THE KEY POWERS OF GOVERNMENT WERE PRESENT FOR THIS MEETING ABOUT DONALD TRUMP, who was about to move into the White House.

"The officials in the meeting would need to figure out how the investigation [of Carter Page and the Trump campaign] could continue despite the fact that its central focus, Trump, was about to be sworn in as president," wrote Andrew McCarthy for *National Review* (Feb. 15, 2018).

Think about that. THESE HIGHEST OFFICIALS, LED BY OBAMA, WERE STRATEGIZING ABOUT HOW TO CONTINUE AN ILLEGAL INVESTIGATION ON THE NEXT SITTING PRESIDENT, WHO WOULD BE THEIR OWN BOSS!

THIS IS TREASON!

President Obama had said that he *never intervened* in investigations being conducted by the Justice Department and FBI. In an April 2016 interview, he said emphatically: "I do not talk to the attorney general about pending investigations. I do not talk to FBI directors about pending investigations. We have a strict line and always have maintained it."

THAT WAS AN EGREGIOUS, MONSTROUS LIE! Obama ruled over those people like a tyrant. They swooned over him, but they also *feared* him.

McCarthy continued, "Obama officials claimed to adhere to a book that forbade consultations between political leaders and investigators. But here they were consulting." And what were they consulting about in that crucial January 5 meeting? How to keep the investigation of Donald Trump going even after he became president! And it was all based on a fraudulent premise of political propaganda.

Could there be a more deadly treasonous act?

SECRETS AGAINST THE PRESIDENT-ELECT

After that meeting, Obama further met with Yates and Comey, both of whom would remain in office after Mr. Trump became president. At this second meeting, President Obama talked about the briefing FBI Director Comey would give the incoming president the next day, January 6. Obama instructed Comey to be selective when he briefed President-elect Trump. Comey was not to tell Trump the truth: that *he* was being investigated.

When Comey briefed Mr. Trump on the Steele dossier, it is almost certain that he described only a *sliver* of it—the embarrassing sexual allegations—so the incoming president would authorize the investigation to continue and to clear his name. Comey must have left out the part about collusion between the Trump campaign and Russians because there is no way Mr. Trump would have approved an investigation that considered him a criminal suspect!

"The main purpose of counterintelligence operations is to keep the president informed," McCarthy wrote, "but when it came to the incoming president, *law enforcement leaders treated the Russia investigation like a criminal probe in which Trump was a suspect. ...*

"Since Trump would have the power to shut down the investigation, the trick was to avoid making him feel threatened by it. Therefore, the strategy was to withhold information that illustrated Trump's centrality to the investigation, assure him that he was not a suspect, and gently admonish him about the need to respect law enforcement's independence (on pain of being accused of obstruction)" (ibid; emphasis his).

Comey told Mr. Trump in private that he was not under investigation. Mr. Trump wanted Comey to relay that message to the public, but he refused—*because it was a despicable lie!* Comey's FBI was actually trying to *find* some crime to justify overthrowing the incoming president!

Imagine this man treating the president-elect this way. And remember, HE WAS SENT BY BARACK OBAMA.

Mr. Trump later fired Comey for this. It is the president's *right* to receive a full briefing of all ongoing investigations. But corrupt agents were withholding vital intelligence from the president and even *spying* on him.

Merriam-Webster Dictionary defines *treason* as "the offense of attempting by overt acts to overthrow the government of the state ...." You don't have to know a lot about government to know that ATTEMPTING TO REMOVE A LAWFULLY ELECTED PRESIDENT FROM OFFICE USING UNVERIFIED PROPAGANDA SO YOU CAN ADVANCE YOUR RADICAL POLITICAL AGENDA IS TREASON OF THE HIGHEST ORDER! Corrupt law enforcement officials, led by Barack Obama and with the help of Hillary Clinton, conspired to overthrow the government of the United States! If that is not treason, then what is?

In America's past history, people guilty of such crimes would have been executed!

About these January 2017 events, journalist Mollie Hemingway wrote, "Not only was information on Russia not fully shared with the incoming Trump team, AS OBAMA DIRECTED, the leaks and ambushes made the transition chaotic, scared quality individuals away from working in the administration, made effective governance almost impossible, and materially damaged national security" (*New York Post*, May 10, 2020).

Two weeks later, on January 20, 2017, Rice wrote an e-mail to herself documenting what happened in the January 5 meeting. This e-mail was odd. As McCarthy wrote, this wasn't really "an e-mail-to-self. It is quite consciously an *e-mail for the record*" (op cit; emphasis his). In it, Rice wrote that everything in the January 5 meeting was entirely aboveboard. President Obama, she wrote, did everything "by the book." The truth is, as McCarthy wrote, Rice's e-mail was "not written to memorialize what was decided. It is written to *revise* the memory of what was decided in order to rationalize what was then done" (emphasis his).

Rice knew that what they had discussed was illegal. She wanted to preempt any investigation by creating a record that everything Obama and the others decided was totally lawful.*

Not one of these elites dared to speak against Obama. Not one! They were in a swooning, fearful trance under Obama's tyrannical leadership.

Only a brazen, lawless, powerful Barack Obama could have led this most treasonous act in U.S. presidential history!

THE NUNES MEMO

On January 16, 2018, Devin Nunes, chairman of the House Intelligence Committee, wrote a letter known as the Nunes memo. The radical-left Democrats in Congress immediately attacked it with fervor. House Minority Leader Nancy Pelosi called it a sham; Senate Minority Leader Chuck Schumer said Nunes was sowing a conspiracy. They fought against the release of the memo and never admitted wrongdoing. But they knew they were lying and that what Nunes had written was absolutely correct.

On February 2, 2018, the House Intelligence Committee released the memo to the public. It exposed terrible corruption inside the FBI and the Justice Department—and a *conspiracy* to undermine Donald Trump. It showed that top FBI and DOJ officials knew the Steele dossier was "salacious and unverified," as Comey put it, but still presented it to the FISA court as if it were proof of a legitimate foreign threat to obtain a warrant to spy on Carter Page.

A September 23, 2016, Yahoo News article about a trip to Moscow that Carter Page took in July 2016 relied extensively on the Steele dossier. The writer received information from Steele directly, so the article does not substantiate the

---

* If you have access to the Internet, I encourage you to read "What Did Comey Tell President Trump About the Steele Dossier?", by Andrew McCarthy in *National Review,* as well as "Obama Meeting Could Be Behind Corrupt Michael Flynn Probe," by Mollie Hemingway in the *New York Post.*

dossier's veracity. Still, the FBI and DOJ included this article in its request for the FISA warrant.

Think about that: A law enforcement source fed information to the media, then the law enforcement agencies used the media's stories as proof that the source was right! The media wrote stories about these claims, which law enforcement agencies used as even more proof to renew the warrant. Law enforcement and the media formed an *echo chamber.*

Mainstream media executives were complicit in this lawless plot. They continually gave credibility to this nonsense.

Lawless, Constitution-hating people now lead our federal law enforcement agencies. They act as if they are superior to Congress, but the Constitution stipulates that Congress must oversee them, otherwise they have no accountability to the American people.

The *New York Times* illegally released the confidential Pentagon Papers in 1971. But this newspaper and the *Washington Post* lobbied hard to prevent the release of the Nunes memo, which is completely legal. *Why the double standard?*

These agencies are supposed to uphold and enforce the law. But this plot proves that they are willing to *trample* on the law to advance a certain radical agenda.

IF THESE LAW ENFORCEMENT AGENCIES CAN ILLEGALLY SURVEIL THE PRESIDENT, WHAT CAN THEY DO TO YOU?

According to the Nunes memo, former FBI Deputy Director Andrew McCabe—who resigned just four days before the memo was released—admitted that, if not for this dossier, there would have been no Russia investigation! STEELE'S DOSSIER ALLOWED THE JUSTICE DEPARTMENT TO APPOINT A SPECIAL COUNSEL, ROBERT MUELLER AND HIS TEAM OF RADICALS, TO COMMENCE THE RUSSIA INVESTIGATION.

James Clapper also later said this investigation WOULD NOT HAVE HAPPENED IF NOT FOR BARACK OBAMA. Clapper said THE WHOLE RUSSIA-TRUMP INVESTIGATION WAS THANKS TO OBAMA. Clearly, MR. OBAMA WAS THE STRONG LEADER OF THESE REBELS. In truth, *so many* lawless, treasonous acts that have wreaked such destruction on our government and our nation would not have occurred if not for Obama! Where does he get all that power? That is something to ponder.

RANK LAWBREAKING

The Trump-Russia investigation lasted *two years* and cost $40 million. The radical left did all they could to use it to cripple the Trump presidency. The *entire investigation* was based on that filthy, worthless dossier and was thus totally fraudulent! It was all to attack Donald Trump and, perhaps more importantly, to distract from and COVER UP THEIR OWN CRIMINAL, TREASONOUS ACTIVITY. Robert Mueller's team knew it was a hoax before they even began the investigation!

They weren't merely trying to wrest control from Mr. Trump—THEY WANTED TO TAKE CONTROL OF THE GOVERNMENT PERMANENTLY. Even today they are working hard to smash the last remaining obstacles preventing them from accumulating so much power over the country that no one can do a thing about it.

Remarkably, in that whole time, NOT ONE PERSON from the Obama administration ever leaked the truth about this fraudulent, treasonous investigation. That too shows how much people fear Barack Obama. Even the Republicans went along with it. Perhaps many of them were guilty of corruption themselves. But certainly all of them, almost to a man, lacked the courage to stand up or speak out. Where have we seen even one serious whistle-blower among these pathetic elites, or anybody else?

OBAMA WIELDS A POWER THAT IS BEYOND HUMAN.

The December 2019 report from Horowitz outlined *17 errors* Comey's FBI committed in launching the Trump-Russia investigation. These were not mere errors—they were treasonous crimes!

The American people are still learning the full extent to which Barack Obama was personally directing this treasonous plot against Donald Trump. And the only reason we know as much as we do is because Devin Nunes pressured the FBI into providing congressional committees with 384 pages of text messages between FBI special agent Peter Strzok, who was leading Crossfire Hurricane, and the woman with whom he was committing adultery, Lisa Page, who was working as counsel to McCabe.*

The text messages between these two FBI operatives revealed shocking antipathy for candidate Donald Trump. Strzok clearly hated Trump. He sent Page a now-infamous message saying that Mr. Trump would never become president, writing: "No. No he won't. We'll stop it."**

But far more importantly, these texts show that the 17 crimes outlined in the Horowitz report were not just the result of some overzealous FBI intern. They reveal that the entire Russia-Trump investigation was being driven from the *very top.*

'THE WHITE HOUSE IS RUNNING THIS'

In his book *Ball of Collusion*, Andrew McCarthy writes that on August 5, 2016, Strzok and Page "had a tense conversation about an imminent meeting involving 'agency people'—apparently

---

* Several people fought for the release of those texts for a long time. The FBI turned them over to Congress on January 16, 2018. That is a significant date (you can read why in our booklet *January 16: God's Miracle Day*) showing that *God was intervening* to make this information public to prevent these people from *blotting out the name of Israel.*

** Strzok also played a leading role in the FBI's investigation of Hillary Clinton, who, while serving as secretary of state, illegally sent, received and deleted 33,000 e-mails from an illicit server that was vulnerable to hacking. What was she hiding? Many of these messages were top secret. Yet the FBI let her off with no consequences.

the CIA." At this meeting, one official—whose name has been redacted in government memos—told FBI officials, "THE WHITE HOUSE IS RUNNING THIS." According to McCarthy, that official was Director Brennan. He was the czar of the president and perhaps the most powerful radical in the government after Obama himself.

"The White House is running this." Brennan made clear WHOSE WILL everyone was to follow: Barack Obama's.

On another occasion, Page said she was preparing certain information for Comey because "POTUS [President of the United States Barack Obama] wants to know everything we're doing."

President Obama said he stayed out of Justice Department investigations. Why? Because involvement in those investigations would open the door to abuse of power, and he didn't want to appear to be abusing his power. But he was *deeply* involved in investigations and *egregiously* abusing his power! He was directing the whole Trump investigation. He *chose* Peter Strzok for that job, a man who had made clear how much he hated Donald Trump and was determined to keep him from the presidency. The fact that *this* was who Obama wanted overseeing the investigation shows how satanic that whole process was! Obama wanted Trump destroyed. And he told these investigators to bring everything related to this matter to him personally.

This is corruption on the deepest level—so deep that most people won't even *believe* it!

Before the 2016 election, just about everyone believed Hillary Clinton would be the next president. Had she won, none of this corruption would have come to light!

We must see the spiritual dimension here. Ephesians 6:12 says, "For we wrestle not against flesh and blood, but against principalities, against powers, against the rulers of the darkness of this world, against spiritual wickedness in high places." The Bible is full of such scriptures. Will we believe them?

Just as Satan comes as an "angel of light," the people he works through appear as "the ministers of righteousness" (2 Corinthians 11:15). But they work in darkness and secrecy.

The radical left is LAWLESS! *They are satanically sick.* These people no longer deal in logic or truth because THEY HAVE BEEN OVERWHELMED BY THE DEVIL.

'IN CRIMINAL JEOPARDY'

Based on the ongoing investigation of Special Counsel John Durham, on September 17, 2021, a grand jury indicted Michael Sussmann, a former Clinton campaign lawyer, for lying to the FBI three weeks before the 2016 election. Sussmann had claimed that the Trump organization was working with a Russian bank with links to the Russian government, and he said he was volunteering this information as a good citizen, not a paid political operative. But Sussmann's billing records show he was working for the Clinton campaign, a tech executive and an Internet company—identified as Rodney Joffe and Neustar, a major company that directs Internet traffic. Prosecutors have in evidence an e-mail from Joffe saying that he was tentatively offered a top cybersecurity post "by the Democrats when it looked like they'd win."

Durham's motion said Joffe led an effort to search web traffic that could connect Donald Trump to Russia. He then passed information to Sussmann, who gave it to the FBI. According to the FBI's internal messaging system, agent Joseph Pientka wrote, "People on the 7th floor [FBI leadership] to include the director are fired up about this server." The FBI wants the public to believe it was duped by Sussmann's lie and didn't know he was working for the Clinton campaign. Sussmann's allegation—that Trump servers were communicating with Russian servers—was easily disproved by the FBI field office in Chicago, and top FBI leadership probably already knew it was bogus. According to the *Washington Times,* "Top bureau officials sent an electronic communication [to field agents] marking the opening of the case and saying the investigation was based on a 'referral' from the Justice Department rather than a tip from Michael Sussmann" (May 23, 2022). Why would FBI leadership try to hide the real source of the material? Probably because everyone in the FBI knew who Sussmann was working for. After investigating the Trump-server allegations, the Chicago field agents said it "lacked merit," "did not pass analytical muster," and did not show a "covert communication system." Nevertheless, FBI top brass pressed ahead.

Even after Trump had taken office, Sussmann provided "an updated set of allegations" to a different U.S. intelligence agency, presumably the CIA. In fact, Durham's April 15, 2022, motion details how Sussmann collaborated with both Fusion GPS and the CIA. So the CIA knew the allegations against Trump were part of a political smear campaign but still let the media use them to try to bring down President Trump.

On November 4, 2021, Durham indicted Igor Danchenko, the principal sub-source for the Steele dossier. These were telling, high-profile charges that suggested the range of Durham's probe.

This law firm hired by Hillary Clinton's campaign, Fusion GPS and the DNC spent *millions of dollars* on the Steele dossier to perpetuate the biggest fraud in American history! Aside from all the other trouble Clinton should be in, spending money donated to her campaign to finance a fraudulent report to smear her opponent violates campaign-finance laws. They know that, which is why they set up so many firewalls to shield themselves. The DNC didn't *technically* fund it—Sussmann's firm, Perkins Coie, did.

Mr. Trump correctly said Durham's filing "provides indisputable evidence that my campaign and presidency were spied on by operatives paid by the Hillary Clinton campaign in an effort to develop a completely fabricated connection to Russia. This is a scandal far greater in scope and magnitude than

Watergate, and those who were involved in and knew about this spying operation should be subject to criminal prosecution. In a stronger period of time in our country, this crime would have been punishable by death." I agree with him entirely.*

This explosive information further exposed the treason committed by top Democrats. *Yet the mainstream press ignored it.* That is shameful complicity with these crimes that are destroying our constitutional republic!

Practically the only media personality willing to touch this story was Fox News host Maria Bartiromo. In November 2021, after the Danchenko indictment, she interviewed Ratcliffe about it.

In that interview, Ratcliffe said that "everything related to the Steele dossier was known to be untrue but yet it was the predicate for moving forward with an unjust, unfair and ultimately ... a criminally negligent investigation against the

---

* On May 31, 2022, Michael Sussmann was acquitted by a Washington, D.C., jury. His acquittal was predicted by many conservatives simply because the case was being tried in heavily Democratic D.C. by a judge with strong ties to Barack Obama. One of the jurors' children is on the same sports team as Sussmann's daughter. Following the case, one juror said, "There are bigger things that affect the nation than a possible lie to the FBI." Nevertheless, Durham's case against Sussmann led to some of the most scandalous revelations about the government's illegal activity against Donald Trump and his campaign. Government contractors obtained Internet traffic data from several of Trump's business and residential properties. Rodney Joffe and these contractors intentionally misrepresented what the data proved and went on to peddle that disinformation to the FBI and media. Filings in the Sussmann case also revealed that Hillary Clinton was aware of the smear campaign, and that the FBI was not "duped" by Sussmann but was in fact working alongside him—literally. Sussmann had his own key card to FBI headquarters, and the FBI had its own office within Sussmann's law firm, Perkins Coie. In the end, the trial proved to be about a much bigger story than the lie Sussmann told the FBI: It proved that the Clinton campaign and Obama's FBI were working together to spy on and smear Donald Trump.

Trump campaign." He said FBI Director Christopher Wray admitted under oath that there was no cause for the FBI to go to the FISA court to seek a warrant to spy on the Trump campaign, yet the FBI did it anyway. Then it continued to spy even after he became president. And crucially, we now know that BRENNAN BRIEFED BOTH OBAMA AND BIDEN ABOUT THIS IN AUGUST 2016, THREE MONTHS BEFORE THE ELECTION. So they *knew* the dossier was fraudulent and that the entire spying operation was based on it.

Ratcliffe said he briefed Rep. Adam Schiff on these exact facts and told him the evidence went all the way up to Obama. Schiff, a radical leftist, immediately went out and publicly said that Trump colluded with Russia and that he had evidence of it! That is the way leftists routinely lie. They are brazen like demons! And virtually nobody holds them accountable. As the Prophet Isaiah wrote, "[J]udgment is turned away backward, and justice standeth afar off: for truth is fallen in the street, and equity cannot enter" (Isaiah 59:14).

Ratcliffe said twice that the documents he provided to Durham reach *the highest levels of government.* He said he knows Durham is looking into this and that those documents reveal "criminal activity that would be the basis for further indictments." He said that a *grand jury* found that "what happened with the Steele dossier ... was criminal in nature." YES IT WAS! "I continue to think there are going to be MANY INDICTMENTS based on the intelligence that I gave to John Durham and that I have seen," he said.

Ratcliffe told Bartiromo that "EVERYONE associated with the Steele dossier, with its creation, its peddling to the FBI, and its use by law enforcement authorities against the Trump campaign ... IS IN CRIMINAL JEOPARDY RIGHT NOW."

That interview with Ratcliffe stunned me. I thought these amazing revelations would spread through the news outlets like a shock wave. This information could not be more significant! It is about TREASON AGAINST OUR COUNTRY and the very FUTURE

OF FREEDOM IN AMERICA. Yet news executives and anchors were and are uninterested.

ALMOST NO ONE HAS THE COURAGE TO SPEAK OUT AGAINST BARACK OBAMA!

In that same interview, Ratcliffe said, "The truth will defend itself." That is true, but we have seen and are seeing that if no one loves the truth and *fights* for it, the truth can be cast down and trampled.

ALL ROADS LEAD TO ...

Bartiromo also interviewed former Department of Defense official Kash Patel. Patel noted Durham's indictments of Sussmann and Danchenko, along with another in August 2020 that links back to the FBI: attorney Kevin Clinesmith, who pled guilty in January 2021 to falsifying records for the FISA court. He pointed out several connections showing how deep the Democratic Party's involvement in these crimes was.

Yet even the interview with Patel betrayed some of the bias and fearfulness to name Obama. Patel said, "All roads lead to Andy McCabe." Yes, McCabe was in the thick of the treasonous lying, even to Inspector General Horowitz. And as Patel said, Clinesmith, the mid-level FBI attorney who was actually indicted, could not "pull off the greatest political scandal in history alone"—he had help from his supervisors. But do you think all roads lead to *Andy McCabe?*

No, they lead to someone much higher. In fact, the Horowitz report reveals that McCabe told the inspector general that the FBI sent the Steele report to President Obama because OBAMA HAD REQUESTED "EVERYTHING YOU HAVE RELEVANT TO THIS TOPIC OF RUSSIAN INFLUENCE." Of course, there *was* no Russian influence, and McCabe knew it—but he was willfully going along, heeding the will of Barack Obama.

Where do all roads lead? Only one person had the all-consuming motive and malice. Only one person had the forceful, dominating will. Only one person had the necessary ring of powerful accomplices in the government and in the media. Only one person had and has the unassailable pride and power to accomplish this ongoing treason against the United States of America. HE MUST BE NAMED! THAT MAN IS BARACK OBAMA.

Even Fox News mostly avoids this subject and says vague things like these indictments could be "bad news for the Clintons." That is hardly speaking out against this terrible evil. Conservatives are too faint of heart! They say they have the courage to tell the truth, but something restrains them from telling the whole truth. They never want to go after the one at the top, even though the future of our country is at stake!

Sadly, even the Horowitz report talks about Obama very little and implicates him in NOTHING! THIS DESPITE ALL THE CLEAR EVIDENCE OF THOSE TWO MEETINGS—January 5 and 6—SHOWING OBAMA WAS IN CHARGE AND IMPLEMENTED A PLAN TO KEEP THE INVESTIGATION GOING EVEN AFTER TRUMP BECAME PRESIDENT. Of course, Obama put Horowitz into his office. In the end, Horowitz said, "We did not find documentary or testimonial evidence that political bias or improper motivation influenced the FBI's decision to [seek FISA authority on Carter Page]." In other words, they *didn't confess* that they were biased. This language is designed to deceive. And of course, the media reported that Horowitz found no bias, and most people just believed it. Horowitz acknowledged that the FBI committed 17 errors (which were actually 17 treasonous acts) but said in effect that its motives for this treason could have been unbiased. What folly!

NATIONAL SURVIVAL AT STAKE

We are in a bitterly *weak* time in America. Lawmakers, judges, bureaucrats and others wielding power are shockingly corrupt. Our institutions are crumbling. Our constitutional form of government is almost completely destroyed.

The evidence shows a tremendous amount of lawbreaking by bureaucrats in intelligence and law enforcement. It shows that PRESIDENT OBAMA FILLED AMERICA'S LAW ENFORCEMENT AGENCIES WITH TREASONOUS AGENTS. It shows that Obama spent his final days in office working with "deep state" operatives figuring out how he could continue to undermine and even spy on the incoming president. Something diabolical was going on until Mr. Trump was elected—and it continued behind the scenes *during* his presidency.

Shamefully, the media were almost completely silent about this story. Why aren't they interested? Could anything be more important? This is about losing our country! This is about going from great freedom to the worst kind of tyranny. But in far too many cases, these newsmakers are *complicit.*

These events gave us a hard look at what radical leftists are willing to do to seize power and stay in power. They have no respect for the rule of law. They believe they are *above* the law. Such contempt for the nation's founding principles is a grave threat to the republic! NO NATION CAN SURVIVE SUCH LAWLESSNESS.

CHAPTER FIVE

BARACK OBAMA AND THE TWITTER FILES

I N 2013, WHEN I FIRST WROTE *AMERICA UNDER ATTACK,* PEOPLE were beginning to wonder what was happening to the United States. By now, many realize that its principles, identity, history and future are indeed *under attack.* Barack Obama worked and is still working to *destroy* America as a constitutional republic. Yet even at this late stage, ALMOST NO ONE IS WILLING TO NAME THE MAN LEADING THIS ATTACK!

One of the few authors who traces America's self-destruction back to its perpetrator is Mark Bradman, who goes by the name Sundance, posting on the blog Conservative Treehouse. He has shown how obvious it is that Obama is the power behind the current Joe Biden regime.

'THE ONE'

The Twitter Files are a series of revelations released beginning in December 2022 by new Twitter owner Elon Musk and a number of journalists he has worked with. They show the secret communications of radical leftists at Twitter and in the government to control people in America and elsewhere by controlling the information they see.

Twitter Files 8.0 contained this key statement from journalist Lee Fang about the secret communications that he was provided and published: "The searches were carried out by a Twitter attorney, so what I saw could be limited."

"There's no *'could be'* in that statement," Bradman wrote. "The searches were limited, specifically time limited, putting all of the scrutiny on the timeline when Donald Trump was in office. ... [I]t's public record [that] the use of Twitter and Facebook as a tool to advance U.S. foreign policy began during the Obama administration. There are dozens of mainstream press accounts of Barack Obama and Hillary Clinton reaching out to Twitter and Facebook for support during the '11/'12 Arab Spring. This is not controversial; it happened" (Dec. 20, 2022).

Twitter began in 2006, became popular in 2007, and was an enormously powerful tool for controlling foreign policy *and for controlling Americans* by 2017 when Donald Trump was inaugurated president. What happened in between? The 2009–2017 presidency of Barack Obama! Yet this batch of Twitter Files and apparently all the others so far have specifically avoided revealing what happened during those years!

"Let me be very, very clear," Bradman wrote. "This release of information was filtered to avoid revealing that President Obama was the originator of this activity. ... BARACK OBAMA ESTABLISHED THE PARTNERSHIP BETWEEN GOVERNMENT AND SOCIAL MEDIA, AND WITHIN THIS RELEASE, TWITTER IS PROTECTING BARACK OBAMA.

"This release is so over-the-top-obvious in its intent to protect the Obama legacy that the nature of the [Department of State]/ [Department of Defense] admissions within it become almost secondary" (ibid).

When Twitter Files 8.0 was released, people mostly talked about how Twitter worked with the United States government to spread propaganda. *But what happened between 2009 and 2017 at Obama's Department of State, Department of Defense and other government agencies?* This is an obvious question with a clear answer, yet few will even ask it!

Musk has been responsible for revealing large amounts of important information through the Twitter Files and even fired employees, such as Twitter counsel and former FBI general counsel Jim Baker, who tried to block the information from getting out. Yet he and the current Twitter staff have still not revealed what Barack Obama did! If something as clear and as important as that continues to be kept secret, it shows that these Twitter Files, as much as they reveal, are still failing to fully expose the whole truth! To pull a shroud over the man who *started* all this deceit, deception, theft and lying leaves the MOST IMPORTANT part of the story untold! In fact, it's not an accurate report. It's tainted. Elon Musk is allowing people to stop the searches at 2017 and not give us the big picture, which has to include Obama. He hasn't done that, and I doubt that he will. Still, he *has* given us enough information that we can figure out the big picture.

Twitter Files 8.0 "reveals that Twitter officers are carefully curating information to protect their interests," Bradman wrote. "When information is curated to protect political interests, it puts a question mark behind all prior releases. ...

"Twitter is trying to protect President Obama because, beyond the ideological alignment, the monopolistic social media system—a partnership between the U.S. government and Big Tech—was essentially designed as a purposeful, oligarchal system. As long as each platform oligarch retains the code of omertà, the system survives" (ibid). That code of silence and noncompliance with authorities and outsiders is what is used in the mafia!

"Remaining in alignment with the group is why Twitter lawyers carefully filtered out the trail to former President Barack Obama. THE ONE IS ALWAYS PROTECTED." That is a strong statement. Bradman can see that radical-leftist elites are not just protecting each other, they are specifically protecting "the One." He can see that the elites look to, and in some respects worship, Barack Obama.

Barack Obama is still "the One" leading an effort to *blot out* what America has been, especially anything that remains of its unique founding and its history with God.

POWER

The Twitter Files haven't directly exposed Barack Obama, but they *have* directly exposed an enormous amount of lawlessness among government officials across several federal agencies. And how have the radical elites responded?

FBI leaders, rather than refuting the allegations, simply smeared the messenger. In an official statement they said: "The men and women of the FBI work every day to protect the American public. It is unfortunate that conspiracy theorists and others are feeding the American public misinformation with the sole purpose of attempting to discredit the agency" (Dec. 21, 2022).

Those Twitter Files show the FBI's direct communications with Twitter—and the FBI calls it "misinformation" and those who share it "conspiracy theorists"! That is a satanic lie! They just say it and you're supposed to believe it. They are saying, *That's our will, and anyone who doesn't accept it is crazy!*

These federal agents insist that they are "trying to serve the American people"—when in reality they are actively crushing their freedom of speech and blotting out their constitutional rights! What a diabolical lie!

Twitter Files 9.0 reporter Matt Taibbi wrote, "Twitter had so much contact with so many agencies that executives lost track. *Is today the DOD and tomorrow the FBI? Is it the weekly call or the monthly meeting?* It was dizzying" (Dec. 24, 2022).

Big Tech has become a dominant force in America and, as we will see, elsewhere in the world. This is not an accident or the result of the free market. BIG TECH—ESPECIALLY BIG TECH CONTROLLED BY RADICALS WHO ARE CONTROLLED BY OBAMA—HAS BECOME AN ACTIVE, POWERFUL TOOL TO INTENTIONALLY DESTROY GOVERNMENTS, INCLUDING AMERICA'S!

By controlling information, these companies are controlling outcomes—such as elections—while providing, as Bradman wrote, "the illusion of freedom" (Dec. 25, 2022).

One of the few other writers to pinpoint Obama's role has been Lee Smith. He wrote in the *Tablet:* "[T]he FBI's penetration of Twitter constituted just one part of a much larger intelligence operation—one in which the bureau offshored the machinery it used to interfere in the 2016 election and embedded it within the private sector" (*Tablet*, Jan. 5, 2023). He quoted former State Department official Mike Benz, who said that "cybersecurity became cybercensorship." Smith continued: "[T]he spy services saw social media as a surveillance tool, like FISA."

Smith concluded: "A whole-of-society industry designed to shape elections and censor, propagandize and spy on Americans was never simply a weapon to harm Donald Trump. It was designed to replace the republic."

WHAT IS HAPPENING IN AMERICA RIGHT NOW IS TREASON, TREASON, TREASON! Even worse, it is an attempt to *blot out the name of Israel.*

FEAR

When Obama prepared to leave the White House in 2016, he thought he would be leaving it to another radical liberal, Hillary Clinton, and continue exerting his power. Then Americans shocked the world by voting in Donald Trump, who promised to undo what Obama had done.

Eleven days later, something meaningful occurred. Obama was in Peru at an Asia-Pacific Economic Cooperation conference and pulled Facebook CEO Mark Zuckerberg aside. He criticized him severely for not doing more to keep "Russian disinformation" off Facebook. That accusation was a lie: Russian disinformation did *nothing* to get Trump elected. Obama was telling Zuckerberg he should have found a way to help stop Trump, like Twitter ultimately did in 2020.

Zuckerberg seems to have gotten the message. He spent more than $400 million as part of the successful effort to oust Trump in 2020.

Consider the power Barack Obama wields! ZUCKERBERG IS ONE OF THE WORLD'S TOP CEOS AND WEALTHIEST MEN, YET HE IS FIERCELY

AFRAID OF OBAMA! Such men, with all their money and power, are not actually free. They *must* be dedicated and loyal to Obama—or else! They are not working *with* Obama; he *controls them.*

With control of the mainstream media, Barack Obama has monstrous influence. With all those people helping him in his agenda, you see that America has become some kind of tyranny— *no longer* a democratic republic. They try to convince people they are fighting for freedom—while pushing the nation into tyranny!

'EGYPT WAS THE TEST'

Remember the 2010–2012 Arab Spring uprisings. Egypt was a strong ally of America in the Middle East. It had also enjoyed good relations with the Jewish nation, Israel, for more than 30 years. Meanwhile, Iran was becoming a more and more dangerous threat: pursuing a policy of Islamic terrorism, threatening oil shipments, and obtaining nuclear weapons. The U.S., Egypt, Israel and other nations all wanted to contain that threat.

Then Barack Obama was elected president. Within five months of taking office, he traveled to Cairo, Egypt, to give a major speech. In it, he altered America's stance toward Islamism, treated Israel's prime minister disgracefully, and gave Iran's terrorist-sponsoring regime a path not only to remain in power over Iranians (many of whom were protesting against the regime) but also to obtain nuclear weapons!

The U.S. and Israel had been relying on Egyptian President Hosni Mubarak to help keep the Middle East from deteriorating. He was an effective leader and a friend of Israel, like his predecessor, the great Anwar Sadat. But Obama's plan was, in the words of his top spy John Brennan, to make Mubarak "toast."

In 2011, Egyptians were protesting against Mubarak's regime, agitating for a better government. Mubarak sought to hold onto power. BUT THEN BARACK OBAMA PHONED HIM. AFTER THAT CONVERSATION, MUBARAK DECIDED TO GIVE UP.

Obama was clearing a U.S. ally out of the way so the terrorist

Muslim Brotherhood could seize Egypt. And he didn't stop at making a phone call.

"The Obama administration first created the public-private partnership with Twitter and Facebook to support the 'Arab Spring' uprising," Bradman wrote (Dec. 20, 2022).

Here is something that happened between 2009 and 2017! *Here* is something we should be seeing Twitter Files about. The tyranny that has seized America has interfered in politics and overthrown leaders before! Who helped overthrow Mubarak in 2011 to help enemies of the U.S.? Who stole the U.S. presidential election in 2020 to help enemies of the U.S.? This power can destroy *nations* by controlling information, technology and uprisings.

Social media proved to be decisive in Egypt's protests, as well as those of several other Middle Eastern states. As Saleem Kassim wrote for Mic back in 2012, "Being capable of sharing an immense amount of uncensored and accurate information throughout social networking sites has contributed to the cause of many Arab Spring activists. Through social networking sites, Arab Spring activists have not only gained the power to overthrow powerful dictatorship, but also helped Arab civilians become aware of the underground communities that exist and are made up of their brothers and others willing to listen to their stories" (July 3, 2012). He described how protests were organized and crowds mobilized through these tools, and he quoted one Egyptian activist saying, "We use Facebook to schedule the protests, Twitter to coordinate, and YouTube to tell the world."

In 2011, the Dubai School of Government released an Arab Social Media Report whose findings, in the words of the *National,* "give empirical heft to the conventional wisdom that Facebook and Twitter abetted if not enabled the historic region-wide uprisings of early 2011" (June 5, 2011). The *National* reported, "Nearly 9 in 10 Egyptians and Tunisians surveyed in March said they were using Facebook to organize protests or spread awareness about them. All but one of the protests called for on Facebook ended up coming to life on the streets" (ibid).

The *Atlantic* reported that social media fulfilled two purposes in these uprisings: "First, Facebook and elsewhere online is where people saw and shared horrifying videos and photographs of state brutality that inspired them to rebel. Second, these sites are where people found out the basic logistics of the protests—where to go and when to show up" (Sept. 3, 2011).

All this was abetted by the Obama State Department! These Big Tech powers can sit over here encouraging "democracy and freedom" while stirring up revolt in the Middle East and literally change the course of history! And they were being directed to do so by Barack Obama.

"As a consequence, Egyptian President Hosni Mubarak was the first elected official to be taken out by former President Obama's deployment of Twitter as a community activist tool for revolution in 2011," Bradman explained (op cit). Obama got what he wanted. The Egyptians who wanted Mubarak out were empowered.

The path was cleared for the Muslim Brotherhood, which had socialist leanings and was assisted by all kinds of militant factions, like al Qaeda, and by the king of terrorism, Iran. The radical Islamists came in and promised the people freedom. Then they gave them the opposite and installed terrorists in the Egyptian government.

Terrorist factions infiltrated the riots and tore down statues and other supposed symbols of oppression. Did they want freedom and democracy? No, they wanted to destroy. They wanted to cancel Egypt's Constitution, attack any form of Christianity, establish sharia law, and work with Iran. They wanted to *blot out the name of Israel.*

Once the new regime was in place, Egyptians realized that they had been hoodwinked, and they rose up against it. The military intervened and got rid of Mohamed Morsi because Egyptians wanted it back the way they had it before.

What is truly amazing, however, is that this plan the Obama administration carried out in Egypt *foreshadowed* a much bigger scheme. As Bradman concluded: "In direct and consequential ways,

EGYPT WAS THE BETA TEST FOR A PROCESS THAT SURFACED A DECADE LATER IN THE UNITED STATES DURING THE 2020 ELECTION" (ibid).

That is a powerful statement. WHAT THEY DID IN EGYPT, THEY THEN DID WITHIN AMERICA!

"Fast-forward to 2020, and those same elements deployed against the Egyptian government were deployed in the United States in a coordinated public-private partnership with Twitter, Facebook and social media," Bradman continued. "The ideological interests between the 2010–'11 'Arab Spring' uprising were the same ideological interests between the 2020 'Black Lives Matter' protests/uprisings. ... The exact same group of U.S. people who were promoting the Mideast Arab Spring in 2010–'11 are the same people who promoted the 2020 Black Lives Matter protests. The same politicians, the same media voices, the same newspapers, the same social media activists. Almost every participant and their support for the uprising ... was identical, including the platforms deployed."

There are direct connections between how Obama's people stirred up revolution in Egypt and how they stirred up revolution in America. The goal in *both cases,* as only the Bible can reveal, was to blot out the name of Israel.

Too few Americans realize it, but their constitutional republic was built on many biblical principles. Obama has cast that to the ground for the same reason that the Antiochus in the Church cast the true doctrines to the ground and for the same reason that the Antiochus in Europe will physically destroy this nation—if we don't repent! They are inspired by the same motivation from the same being!

CONTROLLING ALL THREE BRANCHES

Ceylan Yeginsu wrote a *New York Times* article on December 27, 2017—the year Donald Trump was inaugurated president: "It was a case of the famous interviewing the famous. The BBC aired an interview on Wednesday that was unusual in at least a couple of respects: The man answering the questions was former President Barack Obama, and the man asking them WAS HIS FRIEND PRINCE HARRY. ...

"While neither man mentioned Mr. Trump directly, they discussed the role of social media in leadership, a conversation that brought to mind Mr. Trump's blunt, unvarnished posts on Twitter.

"Mr. Obama warned against the irresponsible use of social media by people in positions of power and expressed his concern about a future in which facts were discarded."

This article then quoted Obama as saying, "One of the dangers of the Internet is that people can have entirely different realities. They can be cocooned in information that reinforces their current biases. THE QUESTION HAS TO DO WITH HOW WE HARNESS THIS TECHNOLOGY IN A WAY THAT ALLOWS A MULTIPLICITY OF VOICES, ALLOWS A DIVERSITY OF VIEWS, but doesn't lead to a Balkanization of society and allows ways of finding common ground."

Does Obama really want "a multiplicity of voices" and "a diversity of views"? Absolutely not! We now know that Barack Obama and his administration got control of Twitter, Big Tech corporations and most of the media. He had Twitter remove Trump's memos and most of those of his supporters—about one half of America! He led Big Tech to do the same.

The extent of this treasonous activity is even worse than you can imagine. As Bradman wrote, "The attempt to remove President Trump from office ENCOMPASSED ALL THREE BRANCHES OF THE U.S. GOVERNMENT.

- "Executive Branch—FBI, DOJ-[National Security Division], CIA, State Department and eventually the Special Counsel Office
- "Legislative Branch—[Senate Select Committee on Intelligence] in 2017 and 2018 with an assist from House Intelligence Committee and House Judiciary in 2019 and 2020
- "Judicial Branch—FISA Court 2015, 2016, 2017; federal judges (Sullivan, Walton, Howell, Berman-Jackson) in alignment with D.C. intents in 2018, 2019 and 2020.

"How does the office of the United States president, and more importantly a constitutional republic itself, survive a coordinated coup effort that involves all three branches of government, while simultaneously those in charge of exposing the corruption fear the scale of the effort is too damaging for the U.S. government to reveal?" (Conservative Treehouse, Jan. 12, 2023).

Treason! Treason! Treason!

HERE WE SEE THAT OBAMA LED ALL THREE BRANCHES OF AMERICA'S GOVERNMENT TO BLOT OUT THE VIEWS OF MR. TRUMP, HIS FOLLOWERS AND OTHER CRITICS.

SEEK GOD

During the Civil War, a time of nightmarish revolt and violence, President Abraham Lincoln said, "Does it not appear strange that men can ignore the moral aspect of this contest?" That "strange" moral ignorance and amorality is far worse today. Corruption is so deep in our government and in our people that it is irreversible without God's help!

Before the Battle of Gettysburg, Lincoln dropped to his knees and prayed to God. How many of our leaders today would do that and submit to their Creator?

Jesus Christ warned that Satan the devil is a murderer and a liar, and that he *controls* people (John 8:44). There is no truth in him—he is utterly amoral. That is how he lives. He rebelled against God and tried to overthrow Him, and God hurled him right back to Earth. Now he is exerting a lot of power—especially through men whose minds are open to him and whom he uses to lie and destroy and murder.

Obama and his helpers in Big Tech and the government wield such power as to "replace the republic," as Lee Smith wrote. His power reaches down to the state and local levels as well. And HE HAS THE GREATEST SPY SYSTEM IN THE WORLD. He has demonstrated that he can target anyone he wants who speaks out about or resists what he is doing—up to and including the legitimately elected and reelected president of the United States! Who's to stop him?

What can they do to you and me? They are already ruining the lives of many Trump supporters. How can anybody fail to recognize that something is dreadfully wrong here?

Americans need to wake up to what is happening and understand that it is motivated and powered by one man in particular. They also need to wake up to understand their Bibles and seek the true God!

Once you forsake God and you lose His protection, you are lost. God is the one who gave us our country. We have forsaken Him, and now He is taking it away. He is letting Satan attempt to blot out its very name.

Our only hope is in the God of the Bible who gave America, Britain, the Jewish state and all the other modern nations of Israel their blessings in the first place. Americans, even religious Americans, need to recognize how far they are from God. They have forsaken God, and that is why Satan has so much power: It is "by reason of transgression" (Daniel 8:12).

Hosea 5:5 prophesies that these three main nations that descended from ancient Israel will fall together. The only way to avoid that is to act on the message of the Bible, the message you are reading right now. There is no other way!

But if you will recognize how far you are from God, if you will hear His message, if you will repent and turn to Him, you will be amazed at the power that comes into your life. You need not be afraid of anything!

CHAPTER SIX

SILENCING
A CRITIC

TWO DAYS AFTER HE WON THE 2016 PRESIDENTIAL ELECTION, Donald Trump met with President Obama in the Oval Office to discuss the transition to the new administration. Of the many issues Mr. Obama could have discussed with Mr. Trump during their 90-minute meeting, he mainly wanted to talk about two people. He told Mr. Trump that the two most dangerous men to be wary of were North Korean dictator Kim Jong-un—*and retired Lt. Gen. Michael Flynn.*

Why was President Obama so concerned with General Flynn? The answer is alarming. And the way Obama treated Flynn gives a chilling picture of how he silences his critics and punishes his enemies.

HOW FLYNN BECAME A TARGET

Many consider Michael Flynn an American hero. He is a decorated war veteran who has saved countless American lives. As an intelligence officer in the Army, he tracked down Islamic terrorists in Iraq and Afghanistan. He was good at his job, and President Obama nominated him as director of the U.S. Defense Intelligence Agency.

In this new office, however, Flynn exposed how the Obama administration was failing to effectively fight the Islamic State and other enemies in the Middle East. He told colleagues that he felt like a lone voice warning that the United States was less safe from radical Islam than it had been before the 9/11 terrorist attacks.

Flynn also criticized Obama for failing to support the enemies of Syrian dictator Bashar Assad, a strong ally of Iran. According to former Defense Intelligence Agency official Patrick Lang, "Flynn incurred the wrath of the White House by insisting on telling the truth about Syria. He thought truth was the best thing, and they shoved him out." Flynn had been on the job for only two years when the Obama administration forced him into early retirement in August 2014.

But telling the truth about Syria was not the only thing that got General Flynn in trouble. He was well educated in intelligence-gathering techniques. This too unnerved Obama officials. They were conducting massive illegal spying operations on American citizens. They must have felt threatened, even after Obama had gained so much control of the spy agencies and the military, that a military hero with access to the intelligence would expose what they were doing. Clearly they were nervous about what Flynn might say, because about a year after forcing him to retire, THEY STARTED TO SPY ON *HIM*.

A former senior Treasury Department official told Star News Group that, starting in December 2015 and continuing well into 2017, Barack Obama's Treasury regularly surveilled Flynn's financial records and transactions. THIS WAS UNLAWFUL, but the Obama administration was obsessed with targeting this man.

And their activities grew still more extreme and lawless. Flynn was one of President Obama's top enemies. The biggest reason, however, wasn't his stance on Syria or his understanding of spying. It was that he was a vocal opponent of Obama's disastrous nuclear deal with Iran.

OBAMA'S IRAN DEAL

The Obama administration implemented its Joint Comprehensive Plan of Action with Iran on January 16, 2016. Under the terms of this agreement, the United States lifted oil and financial sanctions on Iran, while Iran agreed to stop enriching uranium beyond 3.67 percent.

To ensure the deal was completed, on January 17, the Obama administration airlifted $400 million in cash to pay Iran for the release of four innocent American hostages. This was nothing less than a *ransom* payment to a murderous terrorist regime! The U.S. also returned to Iran seven CRIMINALS who were imprisoned or facing charges, and also stopped seeking 14 Iranians who were on Interpol's watch list. According to the *Wall Street Journal,* the cash payment was the first installment of a $1.7 billion settlement the Obama administration agreed to pay Iran.

HOW CAN YOU EXPLAIN AMERICA BECOMING THE NUMBER ONE STATE SPONSOR OF THE NUMBER ONE STATE SPONSOR OF TERRORISM?

America was funding Iran's nuclear aspirations by secretly airlifting that cash payment in the middle of the night. One commentator said you could take that $400 million ransom money and buy four atomic bombs!

General Flynn had left the Obama administration 17 months before, and he was an outspoken critic of the deal. He wrote a 2016 book, *The Field of Fight,* describing correspondence between the Iranian government and al Qaeda leader Osama bin Laden. Apparently al Qaeda was working on chemical and biological weapons in Iran, but the Obama administration refused to declassify the proof.

Flynn also warned that the Russians were cooperating with the Iranians and would probably not help the U.S. fight radical Islamic terrorism. Still, THE OBAMA ADMINISTRATION AGREED TO LET RUSSIA EXPORT CLOSE TO 130 TONS OF NATURAL URANIUM TO IRAN—ENOUGH TO MAKE 10 NUCLEAR BOMBS!

The whole message the Obama administration was peddling about the Iran deal was that it would prevent this radical Islamist regime from getting a nuclear bomb. YET IT COLLUDED WITH RUSSIA TO GIVE IRAN 130 TONS OF URANIUM. How do you explain that? How could the American public be so ignorant as to allow such evil and disastrous foreign-policy decisions?

General Flynn condemned Iran as the "world's leading state sponsor of terrorism" and criticized the Obama administration for cozying up to it. He advocated a strategy aimed at overthrowing the Iranian government.

Then General Flynn did something that made him an even greater enemy: He signed on to help with Donald Trump's presidential campaign. This prompted Obama's FBI to open a counterintelligence investigation against Flynn in August 2016 in hopes of smearing him as a Russian agent.

SPYING ON FLYNN

The people investigating Michael Flynn found nothing—no evidence of any wrongdoing. Internal messages from FBI employees later filed in court showed they had reservations about the probe; one called it a "nightmare." They planned to close the case shortly after the 2016 election.

But then, after winning the election, President-elect Trump appointed Flynn as his national security adviser. So top FBI officials made sure the Flynn investigation stayed open. These officials needed a weapon against Flynn to keep him from discovering what Obama's spymasters and the Justice Department had been doing.

Court filings in Flynn's criminal case show that Peter Strzok texted an unnamed associate on January 4, 2017, "Hey if you haven't closed RAZOR, don't do so yet." Crossfire Razor was the code name for the Flynn probe. Strzok's order was delivered at the behest of FBI leadership.

And when Flynn, in his capacity as incoming national security adviser, began speaking with representatives of foreign governments, *Obama and his top brass were listening in.*

Lee Smith explained this in an article for *Tablet,* "How Russiagate Began With Obama's Iran Deal Domestic

Spying Campaign." "Why were officials from the [Obama] administration intercepting [Flynn's] phone calls with the Russian ambassador?" he asked. "The answer is that Obama saw Flynn as a signal threat to his legacy, which was rooted in his July 2015 nuclear agreement with Iran—the Joint Comprehensive Plan of Action (JCPOA). Flynn had said long before he signed on with the Trump campaign that it was a catastrophe to realign American interests with those of a terror state. And now that the candidate he'd advised was the new president-elect, Flynn was in a position to help undo the deal" (May 20, 2020).

In other words, the smear campaign against Flynn had nothing to do with Russia. It was all about stopping Flynn from helping President Trump undo the Obama administration's Iran nuclear deal.

Then came the infamous January 5, 2017, meeting in the Oval Office where Brennan, Comey, Clapper, Rice, Yates and Rogers briefed Obama and Biden regarding the election and Russian interference. Then came President Obama's follow-on meeting with Biden, Comey, Rice and Yates.

The Justice Department has disclosed handwritten notes from Peter Strzok recounting what Comey had told him about this January 5 follow-on meeting. These notes show that Obama knew details about private conversations between Flynn and Russian Ambassador Sergey Kislyak discussing America's policy in Syria, a UN Security Council resolution about Israel and other subjects. They also reveal that even Deputy Attorney General Sally Yates, Comey's boss, did not know these details. This shows that Obama personally directed this illegal investigation. OBAMA WAS PERSONALLY OVERSEEING THE EFFORT TO TAKE DOWN FLYNN.

You can see why people fear Barack Obama so much: If you cross him, he will come at you with a vengeance!

Strzok's notes recount how Comey told Obama that Flynn's phone calls looked legitimate and that Obama told Comey to "make sure you look at things and have the right people on it." They also record that Vice President Biden brought up the Logan Act—an 18th-century law that forbids private citizens from discussing foreign policy with foreign governments. The law is likely unconstitutional, it has almost never been prosecuted, and it definitely does not apply to national security advisers for incoming presidential administrations. But it ended up being a key weapon against Flynn.

Seven days after the January 5 Oval Office meeting, the *Washington Post*'s David Ignatius published a story about Flynn's contacts with the Russian ambassador. He also specifically raised the nonissue of the Logan Act. How did the *Post* find out about Flynn's phone calls? A "HIGH-RANKING" OBAMA OFFICIAL LEAKED THE TRANSCRIPT TO IGNATIUS, WHICH IS A FELONY.

Nevertheless, the *Post* article triggered the mainstream media and Democratic politicians to focus their attention on Flynn.

Obama administration officials told the public that Michael Flynn had illegally colluded with Russia. This was a brazen lie. There was absolutely nothing wrong with Flynn's phone calls with the Russian ambassador. As another *Washington Post* reporter, Adam Entous, said in October 2017, the newsroom was told that Flynn was having conversations with Ambassador Kislyak, but they didn't assign reporters to it because "[t]here's no reason why he shouldn't be having that conversation."

Entous said that Ignatius could write about it because he was a columnist: "Unlike me as a news reporter, he was able to just throw this piece of red meat out there and just say, 'There was this conversation. What was it about?'"

By getting a commentator to write about the Flynn phone calls, the outgoing Obama administration was igniting media attention and pressuring the incoming administration. Then they set the trap.

The way these government agents can slander and spy on a well-connected American hero like General Flynn shows what they could do to you if they disagreed with your political views.

THE PERJURY TRAP

Flynn may not remember every detail of each phone call he had with the Russian ambassador. Obama's agents, on the other hand, had transcripts and knew what he said better than he did.

The day after the January 12, 2017, *Washington Post* article, the media asked members of President-elect Trump's staff about Flynn's call, particularly about the topic of sanctions. Flynn told his co-workers that he didn't remember discussing sanctions. On January 15, Vice President Mike Pence publicly stated that there had been no talk about economic sanctions between Flynn and the Russian ambassador. Pence said Flynn told him that neither sanctions nor the decision to expel diplomats came up on the call. Transcripts of the call, however, reveal that Flynn spoke to Kislyak about the expulsion of diplomats. But Pence did not have access to transcripts—and neither did Flynn.

Later, in 2020, John Ratcliffe declassified the Flynn transcripts. In all those transcripts, the word "sanction" appears once, and it was brought up by Ambassador Kislyak. The *Federalist*'s Sean Davis wrote: "The transcripts show that while Kislyak obliquely raised the issue of financial sanctions against certain Russian intelligence officials, Flynn himself never discussed the financial sanctions against Russian individuals and entities levied by the Obama administration. Instead, Flynn focused on preventing U.S. 'tit-for-tat' escalation following the Obama administration's expulsion of Russian diplomats" (May 29, 2020).

On January 23, 2017, three days after the inauguration, the *Washington Post* ran an article titled "FBI Reviewed Flynn's Calls With Russian Ambassador but Found Nothing Illicit." There was nothing wrong with his phone calls and everyone knew it. But Obama's agents pushed ahead with their plan to catch Flynn in a lie.

On January 24, the FBI sprang its trap. FBI Director Comey sent Peter Strzok and Joe Pientka to Flynn's office at the White House to conduct an interview with Flynn, two days after he was appointed.

FBI Counterintelligence Chief Bill Priestap wrote a note to the FBI agents who were going to question Flynn, asking: "What's our goal? Truth/Admission or get him to lie, so we can prosecute him or get him fired?" Another note said they were trying to "get him to admit to breaking the Logan Act."

Armed with the transcript of his phone calls, the agents invited themselves into Flynn's office, pretending they were there on a more or less routine visit to check with him about reports in the media. They didn't warn Flynn of what they were doing, as is normal protocol; they bypassed Justice Department and White House protocols.*

Flynn denied having a conversation with Kislyak four weeks earlier about sanctions. The Obama agents characterized this omission as lying to the FBI and actively misleading members of the Trump administration. Some publicly speculated that Flynn would be susceptible to Russian blackmail because of the call.

On January 26, Sally Yates told President Trump's counsel that Flynn made statements to them about sanctions that were untrue. Flynn continued to publicly state that he did not discuss sanctions. Then on February 9, the *Washington Post* wrote about the content of Flynn's phone calls. Citing unnamed "current and former officials," the *Post* reported that Flynn "privately discussed U.S. sanctions against Russia with that country's ambassador to the United States during the month before President Trump took office, contrary to public assertions by Trump officials ...." Not only was this narrative bogus, but disclosing this information to the press was illegal.

This article embarrassed the Trump White House and led to Michael Flynn's forced resignation on February 13. He was ousted after only 22 days in office, much to the relief of Obama's deep state. This was not because of anything he said to the Russian ambassador, but because he made Vice President Pence look

---

* In 2018, James Comey bragged on MSNBC that he just sent these two agents without the required approvals, saying it was something he probably wouldn't have "gotten away with" in a more organized administration. He admitted to taking advantage of the Trump transition.

uninformed or duplicitous for having said what he did about the phone call. The Obama administration holdovers were actively trying to sow chaos in the incoming administration. They achieved their goal, convincing the public that Flynn was trying to cover up some sinister crime with Russian agents. The media loved that story! And they ignored the information about why Flynn was ousted, though the records are all available publicly.

OVER THREE YEARS LATER, IN MAY 2020, THE JUSTICE DEPARTMENT DROPPED ITS CASE AGAINST FLYNN AFTER COURT DOCUMENTS REVEALED THE CASE WAS A SETUP. Flynn's prosecutors admitted that the FBI's interview of General Flynn was "unjustified" and was not "conducted with a legitimate investigative basis." Attorney General William Barr said the FBI's investigation laid "a perjury trap for General Flynn."

But the damage was done. Rather than serving the Trump administration, Flynn was entangled in spurious litigation for years.

THIS WHOLE DISGRACEFUL EPISODE WAS ORCHESTRATED BY BARACK OBAMA TO PROTECT THE IRAN NUCLEAR DEAL.

MORE LIES

On May 12, 2017, *Good Morning America* host George Stephanopoulos asked Joe Biden what he knew about the Flynn investigation. He dogmatically stated, "I know nothing about those moves to investigate Michael Flynn." But then he was pressed about his role in the January 5 meeting. He revised his answer, saying, "I thought you asked me on whether or not I had anything to do with him being prosecuted. I'm sorry. I was aware that ... they had asked for an investigation, but that's all I know about it."

Peter Strzok's handwritten notes have since revealed both statements to be lies. It was Biden who brought up the Logan Act as a possible means of prosecuting General Flynn. The Democrats act like such lies are nothing to be concerned about.

Lying is the *modus operandi* of these Obama-era officials. THEY LIE AS A WAY OF LIFE!

Andrew McCabe testified before the House Intelligence Committee to condemn Flynn for the lies he supposedly told. McCabe, however, was later caught lying by Horowitz about his involvement in leaking information about the FBI's Clinton Foundation investigation to the *Wall Street Journal.**

McCabe is willing to do whatever Barack Obama wants him to do. That is how all these people attached to Obama behave. They are still calling American hero Michael Flynn a clandestine agent of Russia. These officials have been repeatedly exposed for such deception. They believe it is *right* to lie when it advances their agenda and is for an "important purpose." They have no fixed principles. And very few will hold them to account!

This is what the power of Satan and his Antiochus will do. It is frightening.

America's Constitution was made to rule a *moral, self-governing people,* a well-informed people who will hold their leaders to a high moral standard. Ignorant people can never make our Constitution work. The ignorance of the American people regarding what is happening here is disastrous.

A MYSTERY?

Lee Smith wrote a book titled *The Plot Against the President: The True Story of How Congressman Devin Nunes Uncovered the Biggest Political Scandal in U.S. History.* He is an expert on how Obama and his colleagues tried to frame Donald Trump, Michael Flynn and others for crimes they did not commit.

Still, Smith does not understand why Barack Obama so vehemently supported Iran. "It's not hard to see why the previous president [Obama] went after Flynn: The retired general's

---

* According to Michael Horowitz's 2019 report, McCabe lied ("lacked candor") on several occasions to FBI agents and also while under oath. Federal prosecutors recommended charging McCabe, but Attorney General William Barr let him off the hook.

determination to undo the Iran deal was grounded in his own experience in two Middle Eastern theaters of combat, where he saw how Iran murdered Americans and threatened American interests," he writes. "BUT WHY OBAMA WOULD CHOOSE THE ISLAMIC REPUBLIC AS A PARTNER AND ENCOURAGE TACTICS TYPICALLY EMPLOYED BY THIRD WORLD POLICE STATES REMAINS A MYSTERY."

This is a mystery to a sharp analyst like Lee Smith. Almost *all* Americans are mystified by or oblivious to it. But THE BIBLE REVEALS THIS MYSTERY. And those who *do* see it have an obligation to speak out!

THE MYSTERY EXPLAINED

Remember the satanic goal explained in the prophecy of 2 Kings 14:26-27 to "blot out the name of Israel from under heaven." Iran's mullahs publicly say they want to "wipe Israel off the map." That is another way of saying they want to "blot out the name of Israel from under heaven"! WHY IN THE WORLD WOULD AN AMERICAN PRESIDENT ALIGN WITH THESE MURDERERS? WHY PERMIT RUSSIA TO GIVE IRAN 130 TONS OF URANIUM? And why implement a deal that virtually guarantees Iran becomes a nuclear power?

This prophetic passage in 2 Kings 14 explains. President Obama *shares* the goal to "blot out the name of Israel"!

The Iranians may not know that the Americans are literal descendants of ancient Israel, but they do label America "the great Satan" and the Jewish state "the little Satan." They want to *blot these nations out!* And through his Iran nuclear deal, BARACK OBAMA WAS HELPING THEM ACCOMPLISH THIS GOAL. He was implying, *You blot out the Jews, and we'll blot out America. We'll* "*blot out the name of Israel from under heaven" by transforming America into a socialist state its founders wouldn't recognize.* He wants to destroy everything good in America because everything good in this nation traces back to God, the God of Israel. Spiritually, he wants to wipe out the faith of Israel—just like the Iranian mullahs want to wipe Israel off the map.

This is what Lee Smith does not understand. Obama decided to "choose the Islamic Republic as a partner" and to use "tactics typically employed by Third World police states" because he wants to blot out both the Jewish state and America! Like the ancient Seleucid King Antiochus, he is empowered by the devil to destroy the people of Israel through flattery and deceits that lead to violence.

Any man who tries to blot out the name of Israel is a type of Antiochus.

Had God not intervened to save America "by the hand" of Donald Trump, then America's republic would have been blotted out—and Iran's theocracy would probably have a nuclear weapon!

WHAT KIND OF MAN IS THIS?

Daniel's prophecy provides more details about what sort of man this Antiochus is. History also supplies important insight.

Daniel 11:21 says this leader obtained rule through deceitful lies and flatteries. He was a smooth talker and had a compelling personality. George Rawlinson's *A Manual of Ancient History* says, "Antiochus, assisted by Eumenes, drives out Heliodorus, and obtains the throne, 176 B.C. He astonishes his subjects by an affectation of Roman manners." Anciently, Antiochus Epiphanes gained control by pretending to be someone he wasn't. He was a master deceiver. The same is true in this end time.

WE MUST ALWAYS BEWARE OF THE DEVIL FOR THIS REASON: HE COMES AS AN ANGEL OF LIGHT (2 Corinthians 11:14).

Antiochus IV was called Antiochus "Epiphanes," or "God manifest." That is not a good sign. In his later years as he amassed more power, Antiochus grew more evil and maniacal. Seleucid coins minted during his reign actually show a progression into madness. Early in his rule, coins had his portrait and the words "King Antiochus"; this was normal. Later on, his portrait on coins featured a star on his forehead, implying divinity. Toward the end of his reign, as he adopted divine honors, coins were labeled

"King Antiochus, Epiphanes," or "King Antiochus God," and his portrait was idealized into a depiction of the Greek god Apollo, with rays emanating from his head like a crown of light. He was the first Greek king to be thus represented. The last coins in his reign depict him as Zeus, with the label "King Antiochus, God Manifest, Victory-bearer."

Antiochus really believed he was God manifest. That is a frightening belief! This egotistical claim was inspired by the devil. Antiochus became Satan-possessed (Isaiah 14:12-14). Satan had a grip on him and moved him to exact some of the worst evil ever done to the Jewish people.

Polybius, a Greek historian contemporary with Antiochus, wrote in his book *The Histories,* "King Antiochus was both energetic, daring in design, and worthy of the royal dignity." This was a rare compliment from a man who otherwise described Antiochus as insane. We don't have Polybius's complete work, but another Greek historian, Athenaeus of Naucratis, who did, wrote, "Polybius, in the 26th book of his *Histories,* calls him [Antiochus IV] *Epimanes* ('Insane') and not Epiphanes ('Illustrious') because of his acts." Polybius used wordplay on the title Antiochus gave himself to describe him as *insane.* He also said Antiochus "was smitten with madness."

Why did he call Antiochus "insane"? "Because of his acts"— his deeds, his fruits. Polybius judged him by what he did, not what he said.

JUST IMAGINE WHAT THIS MEANS FOR US TODAY. These modern-day Antiochus figures are certainly to be feared. Viewed spiritually, Satan himself is insane! He is the opposite of God and smitten with madness!

THE DEVIL'S FINGERPRINTS

We must be able to recognize the devil's fingerprints on what was taking place with Michael Flynn. As Jesus Christ said of the devil, there is NO TRUTH in him—none! And THE RADICAL LEFT LIE LIKE

THE DEVIL. That is the spirit behind these people who will say and do *anything* to accomplish their goals. The way they worked to destroy the life of Michael Flynn, an upstanding American patriot, is chilling proof. They will stop at nothing to take over the government and align America with the government of Iran and other tyrannical states. EVERY TIME THEY ARE CHALLENGED ON ANYTHING ILLEGAL THEY HAVE DONE, THEY LIE—OVER AND OVER AND OVER AGAIN.

Yet still, when people ask them a question, somehow, no matter how outrageous the answer, they believe them! The spirit of deception is frighteningly deep. These people are influenced by the devil!

Christ also said in John 8:44 that Satan was a murderer "from the beginning." The very first human child grew up to become a murderer: Cain. That first murder in human history was *inspired by the devil.* Consider that! It vividly shows what a deceitful and murderous influence Satan was and is.

The brazen spirit of the radical leftists isn't just politics or even ideology: It is the spirit of Satan the devil. That is the spirit motivating the moral, cultural, social, institutional and political destruction of this country.

Satan's real goal is not merely to attack a certain man or even a nation. He is attacking everything of God!

The real enemy is *not* Barack Obama. Obama's efforts to "blot out Israel" DO NOT COME FROM A MAN—BUT FROM SATAN THE DEVIL!

Why aren't the media sounding the alarm about what is happening? Because they too are deeply complicit in this treasonous activity.

But despite all the power that radical leftists have over government and the media, somehow the truth keeps coming out. It is coming out not because of Republicans or even because of Donald Trump. What you need to realize is that *God* is causing the truth to emerge. He is giving all of us a good look at the truth. Can you recognize it?

CHAPTER SEVEN

AMERICA HAS NO HELPER

AFTER DONALD TRUMP SURPRISED THE ENTIRE POLITICAL AND media establishment by winning the 2016 election, radical leftists launched a treasonous plot to destroy him politically. One of their main weapons was a special counsel, appointed by the Department of Justice in May 2017. Led by Robert Mueller, it was to investigate "interference with the 2016 election."

THIS SPECIAL COUNSEL DID NOT INVESTIGATE THE DEMOCRATS' UNCONSTITUTIONAL AND OTHER ILLEGAL ACTIONS. IT INVESTIGATED THE DULY ELECTED PRESIDENT, DONALD TRUMP.

Probably most everyday Americans did not believe that the Trump campaign colluded with the Russian government to win the 2016 election. At the same time, most probably believed and *still* believe that Robert Mueller was honestly investigating to make sure that was the case. The political elites and mainstream media certainly portrayed it that way.

BUT THAT IS NOT TRUE, as the facts have since proved. And they show that all these powerful people KNEW IT! They all allowed it to go on as part of their own opposition to Mr. Trump and all he stood for.

ROBERT MUELLER'S TWO GOALS

Look again at the prophecy of 2 Kings 14:26: "For the LORD saw that the affliction of Israel was very bitter, for there was none left, bond or free, and *there was none to help Israel*" (Revised Standard

Version). This verse perfectly describes the attack represented by the Mueller investigation.

Consider the facts. President Barack Obama had set up the agenda before leaving office. His administration tried to help Hillary Clinton win the 2016 election. FBI Director James Comey opened an investigation against Donald Trump, continued the investigation after he was inaugurated president, lied about it, and entrapped and forced out Michael Flynn, who would have been in a position to uncover what the leftist deep state had been doing. THE MUELLER INVESTIGATION WAS A WAY TO CONTINUE TARGETING MEMBERS OF THE TRUMP ADMINISTRATION *AND* TO COVER UP THE TRUTH ABOUT WHAT OBAMA AND THE OTHERS HAD DONE AND WERE PLOTTING.

Depending on how you count it, the Department of Justice investigation lasted between 22 months and at least three years—most of the president's first term—before it finally closed. These people spent *years* pressuring, intimidating and spying on those connected to the president. They entrapped his national security adviser; raided the home, office, hotel and safe-deposit boxes of the president's personal lawyer; intimidated dozens of people with indictments and threats of indictments. And in the end, they provided *zero evidence* of collusion between the Trump campaign and Russian operatives. That is because the Trump campaign never colluded with Russia.

All this is now publicly known. But few people have connected the dots to realize just what these facts reveal. Mainstream journalists certainly have not. They have continued *covering for* this fraudulent investigation.

You will only find real insight from analysts outside the mainstream. On the blog Conservative Treehouse, investigative journalist Mark Bradman has connected these dots: "Robert Mueller had two goals as special counsel. Goal No. 1 was to continue the fraudulent DOJ/FBI 'Stop Trump' operation initiated by James Comey, Andrew McCabe and their crew, technically named Crossfire Hurricane. Goal No. 2 was to bury the illegal action; to create the cover-up needed for everything that took place in the 'Stop Trump' operation" (Jan. 30, 2021).

That *second goal* is the one most people have overlooked—but it is most important! The Mueller investigation's goal was not only to keep all the actions against President Trump going, but also to BURY ALL THE ILLEGAL ACTION. We must realize this.

People *knew* that Russian collusion never happened and that Mueller's investigation was actually a political weapon to stop Trump. BRADMAN ASSERTS THAT, IN FACT, *EVERYONE IN WASHINGTON, D.C., KNEW!*

WHO ALL KNEW?

"They all knew." That's how Bradman put it. "Every person in every branch of government and every federal agency knew Mueller's real purpose" (ibid). There was abundant proof of what had been going on under the Obama administration and what the deep state was doing even after President Trump took office. But Mueller and his team used their power to cover it up and make it much harder to find and prove. And everyone permitted it: They allowed an illegal, treasonous attempt to overturn the results of the 2016 election!

THINK OF ALL THE PEOPLE WHO HAD TO COOPERATE for the Mueller probe to be as invasive as it was for as long as it was, and you begin to realize just HOW DEEP THIS CORRUPTION GOES.

As Bradman wrote: "The legislative branch knew. The judicial branch knew. The executive branch knew. The FISA court knew. ... All of the insiders knew the Mueller probe was one big vacuum to suck up all of the evidence that would have exposed a corrupt [depraved] system to We the People.

"THEY DID ALL OF THIS BECAUSE THE SCALE OF THE ORIGINATING SCANDAL WAS SO SEVERE IT WOULD BE ALMOST IMPOSSIBLE FOR OUR NATION TO COPE WITH THE CONSEQUENCES" (ibid).

Everyone involved in permitting that investigation knew they were participating in an illegal, treasonous attempt *to overturn the legitimate results of the 2016 election. That* was the purpose of Mueller's special counsel.

What else could possibly explain an investigation into zero evidence of something that did not happen?

The complicity among the political class, including Democrats, Republicans, the news media and others, is far deeper than Americans realize. The amount of power, money, influence, technology and intimidation they wield is staggering.

We need to be concerned most of all about that second goal: "to bury the illegal action; to create the cover-up needed for everything that took place in the 'Stop Trump' operation."

The deep corruption involved here is now being exposed before our eyes. And it was prophesied in 2 Kings 14:26. This verse gives you an idea of the *extent* of the corruption in Washington. America's affliction is *very bitter,* and *nobody with any power is helping.*

NO HELPER

The late conservative commentator Rush Limbaugh knew Donald Trump. He said he asked him if he was guilty of the accusations that the Mueller investigation was using as a pretext. Mr. Trump said no. He asked if he was *sure.* He said he was absolutely innocent. Mr. Limbaugh then said, *If you know it's false, then they know it too.*

Mueller's special counsel was not a legitimate investigation, Mr. Limbaugh said, and Donald Trump may have been the only one in Washington who didn't realize it! He said he tried as hard as he could to convince the president that the whole operation was a political attack on his presidency. President Trump knew he wasn't guilty of the accusations, but HE COULD NOT BELIEVE THAT THE DEPARTMENT OF JUSTICE AND THE REST OF THE GOVERNMENT WERE SO MASSIVELY CORRUPT.

But it WAS that corrupt! Especially after eight years of Obama forcibly shaping the government. Special Counsel Mueller *knew* no collusion with Russia ever occurred—and almost everybody else knew it, too. The leaders at the Justice Department knew it. The leaders at the FBI knew it. The directors of the intelligence agencies knew it. Members of the congressional committees, both Republican and Democrat, knew it. They all wanted to create the illusion that Mueller's team was looking for the truth, but it never was. They were simply covering up their attempted coup—their TREASON against this nation!

How could radicals keep all their corruption quiet? Why did some Republicans let them? Well, *they all live by an understanding in "the swamp,"* as Washington's political class is often called. The understanding is this: If you don't go along with the way things are done, the established powers will ensure you lose everything! That is why, for example, a Republican congressman characterized Trump supporters as part of a "cult." He accused 75 MILLION AMERICANS of being in a cult—yet he views the way people in the swamp conduct business as good and normal. That is how sick and warped even some Republicans have become.

These people were literally trying to overthrow the government of the land! To see the full picture, Mr. Trump would have had to realize that their goal was to cover up the truth about what they were doing. He would have had to realize that even some of his own lawyers were in on it. Mr. Limbaugh said lawyers like John Dowd were telling the president that the fastest way to make the investigation go away was to cooperate with it. So he did, knowing they would find no Russian collusion. But this made the investigation seem legitimate.

In America, "innocent until proven guilty" is a foundational principle of justice. The burden of proof is on the accuser. If someone accused *you* of colluding with Russia, you wouldn't have to prove that you didn't; the accuser would have to prove that you did. Yet the Justice Department and the government tried to make Donald Trump out to be guilty unless he proved his innocence, in a blatant attempt to dethrone him.

This is what the 2 Kings 14 prophecy is all about. There was no helper for Israel! Do *you* see any help? Now even Rush Limbaugh, a very influential man who was unafraid of exposing the radical-left agenda, has died. There is *nobody*, especially in Washington, who is a helper for Israel! God was using President Trump, but leftists stole the election and he has been politically EXILED! And none of these terribly guilty elites are being prosecuted, much less convicted or imprisoned—because even many of the prosecutors and the judges are corrupt!

We now know that the Justice Department and FBI lied to the FISA court, yet that court never said anything about it. Why is that? Because they are in on it! This shows you the *power* of the radical-left deep state.

Mr. Limbaugh said Trump had trouble accepting how deep the corruption truly goes. But consider it: The radicals control everything—education, the news media, entertainment, social media, spy agencies—and now, much of the federal government! They can protect lawless rioters and steal an election at the same time they block your free speech for saying that the election was stolen. My son's *Trumpet Daily* show has been censored by YouTube.

They impeached President Trump even after he left the White House in an attempt to block him from ever holding office again. Meanwhile, they are rewarding people at the very center of the corruption, like Peter Strzok, with high-paying jobs and back pay.

That is the way things work in the swamp. They have the power and the control. How can you win against that? How can you win if they rig the election itself?

Let's back up and examine how America got to this point.

RECRUITING TECH COMPANIES

In our modern world, digital surveillance and collection plays a huge role in intelligence gathering. International conflict has become a digital battle space, and leaders the world over have grown very dependent on their intelligence services to know what is going on. Those intelligence agencies are becoming the backbone of governments.

The U.S. has some of the most sophisticated intelligence services and data-collection technology in the world. The NSA surveillance database is an extraordinarily powerful tool used by America and its allies. And now the NSA gets a lot of its data from *private technology companies* like Facebook, Twitter, Google and Microsoft. The intelligence apparatus has recruited these firms as crucial partners (see Chapter 5).

Barack Obama has used this partnership to WEAPONIZE America's intelligence services. HE SUCCESSFULLY TOOK A SYSTEM CREATED TO SURVEIL AND NEUTRALIZE THE NATION'S EXTERNAL ENEMIES AND DEPLOYED IT INSTEAD AGAINST HIS POLITICAL ENEMIES WITHIN AMERICA.

Obama effectively created a *new bureaucratic monster* out of the Department of Homeland Security, the Department of Justice, the Federal Bureau of Investigation and the Office of the Director of National Intelligence—a "fourth branch of government" full of unelected deep state bureaucrats who are loyal to him, his ideology and his goals.

"When the intelligence branch within government wants to conduct surveillance and monitor American citizens, they run up against problems due to the Constitution of the United States," wrote Mark Bradman. "They get around those legal limitations by subcontracting the intelligence gathering, the actual data-mining, and allowing outside parties (contractors) to have access to the central database [speaking of the vast NSA database]. The government cannot conduct electronic searches (Fourth Amendment issue) without a warrant; however, private individuals can search and report back as long as they have access" (July 26, 2021).

This means that these agencies can spy on anybody they want to—even on Donald Trump while he was the sitting president! These bureaucrats have the capacity to get into your computer and read everything you write and hear virtually every word you say. You must realize that there is really no privacy anymore and, frankly, no FREEDOM!

These "private" companies now openly admit that they are helping the government's intelligence agencies to monitor all activity in their platforms to identify whatever they consider "extremist content." *They define* extremism—and it happens to be ANYONE WITH OPPOSING POLITICAL VIEWS! If they dislike your views—even if you are the president of the country—they will censor you, blacklist you, harass you, even throw you in jail. They have usurped authority on a scale never before seen in this country.

THIS IS RANK LAWLESSNESS. IT TRAMPLES THE CONSTITUTION, THE SUPREME LAW OF THE LAND!

These companies now have a virtual choke hold on the government—as Obama guides them. THEY HAVE BECOME WEAPONS FOR BARACK OBAMA. That is what it amounts to, even to this day. This undemocratic "fourth branch of government" is out of control, and it controls the other three branches. And *none* of these people doing the dirty work have been elected, other than Barack Obama.

How could we Americans allow this to happen?

CONTROLLING INFORMATION

Of all the intel agencies, the one Obama wanted control over most was the FBI. The FBI does the domestic investigative work on anyone who needs or holds a security clearance, so control over the FBI put him in charge of who can access what information.

To guard against abuse of power, intelligence agencies' "information is purposefully put into containment silos; essentially a formal process to block the flow of information between agencies and between the original branches" of government, Bradman wrote (July 4, 2021). These intelligence bureaucrats can keep their information locked away from elected officials if they choose, and there is virtually no oversight! They decide which "silo" you have access to so you see only the intelligence they want you to see.

The intelligence branch has full control over what is considered classified information. That is why this "fourth branch" has control over the three actual, constitutional branches: executive, legislative and judicial. When other branches ask for intelligence information, often the agencies will provide it with key parts redacted to hide what is really going on. They control that, without oversight. THE ONLY ONES WHO SEE THE WHOLE PICTURE ARE BARACK OBAMA AND HIS TOP MEN.

This gives these people unparalleled control! They had such power that they could keep President Trump out of crucial information and decisions! Over and again, Trump tried to get people into key positions, and these bureaucrats would deny them. They had unchecked control and could stop him.

THIS IS UNCONSTITUTIONAL, ILLEGAL, LAWLESS AND TREASONOUS! It is *unbelievable* they can do this and get away with it, yet that is exactly what they are doing.

WEAPONIZING INTELLIGENCE

One article by Bradman is titled "The Surveillance and Political Spying Operations Highlighted by John Durham Are the Tip of the Iceberg." He is right about that: What we are seeing is only a *fraction* of this monstrous amount of corruption!

"Barack Obama and [Attorney General] Eric Holder did not create a weaponized DOJ and FBI," Bradman wrote; "instead, what they did was take the preexisting system and retool it, so the weapons only targeted one side of the political continuum. Together they recalibrated the domestic surveillance capabilities, the internal spying systems, so that only their political opposition would be targeted" (Feb. 12, 2022). By doing this, they gained control of the whole system, and the fruits prove that. Instead of aiming these powerful tools at terrorists and other enemies outside the country, they aimed it at their political opponents.

These people consider Donald Trump's Republican followers *extremists* who must be scrutinized and investigated. And this new security system they can use against them is extraordinarily powerful.

WHAT THESE PEOPLE ARE DOING IS BRAZENLY TREASONOUS! IT IS AN ALL-OUT WAR AGAINST THE CONSTITUTION. THEY ARE UNIMAGINABLY DEPRAVED. AND THEY HAVE THE BLESSING AND AID OF THE MEDIA AND THE EDUCATIONAL SYSTEM AS WELL. They hate the Constitution and are working to destroy it. If our people knew even a little bit about God and the Bible, they would recognize that.

To ensure legislative oversight of the intelligence community, a "Gang of Eight" was created to include top House and Senate leaders, both Republican and Democrat. The intelligence community is not to carry out intelligence-gathering operations without the majority and minority parties knowing about them—that is against the law. The legislature is authorized to scrutinize the intelligence operations of this "fourth branch." "The modern design of this oversight system was done to keep rogue and/or corrupt intelligence operations from happening," Bradman wrote. "However ... THE PROCESS WAS USURPED DURING THE OBAMA ERA" (ibid).

Comey and his team were investigating Donald Trump for over a year, and these eight members of Congress *never knew it.* When Comey testified before Congress on March 20, 2017, WHY they kept this secret, he arrogantly said it was "because of the sensitivity of the matter." Essentially he said, *We in agencies like the FBI know how to handle it. We don't need oversight!* James Comey was never elected by anybody, and he isn't accountable to the people. *Yet Congress never pressed him on this point.* That is madness. THAT IS INVITING SATAN THE DEVIL TO CONQUER YOU!

Regarding Comey's comment, Bradman wrote, "The arrogance was astounding, and the acceptance by Congress was infuriating. However, that specific example highlighted just how politically corrupt the system had become. In essence, Team Obama usurped the entire design of congressional oversight, and Congress just brushed it off." This represented "the total usurpation of the entire reason the Gang of Eight exists: to eliminate the potential for political weaponization of the intelligence community by the executive branch. The Gang of Eight notifications to the majority and minority of the legislative branch are specifically designed to make sure what James Comey admitted to doing was never supposed to happen" (ibid). This means this "fourth branch of government" can do WHATEVER IT WANTS.

How could this happen? Clearly, the Democrats *liked* what these intel agencies were doing—and *some Republicans did as well.* Many of them were themselves corrupt!

How alarming that America has no leaders willing to stand up for THE TRUTH. Everybody *fears* Barack Obama—and they dislike Donald Trump, including most Republicans.

It is BITTER to see elected representatives in Congress allow some unelected, arrogant, satanic cabal to take over our country. It is infuriating to have a tyrant ruling the intelligence agencies and the three constitutional branches. Now these people are working hard to stop all state-level election reform efforts and to remove constitutional protections so they can steal elections!

This compliant Congress apparently will bend to anything or anyone that has real power. With precious few exceptions, they will not stand up because they fear retribution. "Not a single person in power will say openly what has taken place," Bradman wrote. "They are scared of the fourth branch. The evidence of what has taken place is right there in front of our face" (ibid). This man can see it.

These federal agencies were spying on Americans en masse. That included everyday Americans, journalists, conservatives, members of the Trump campaign and even sitting members of Congress! In 2016, there was a 350 percent increase in official requests to unmask the identities of Americans whose communications and other details the government was tracking. YOU KNOW THEY FOUND A LOT OF INCRIMINATING INFORMATION AND USED IT TO BLACKMAIL PEOPLE. Is that why so many people have remained silent about all this criminal activity? That is the kind of world we live in.

A democracy that is run like this cannot last long. If Americans do not *love* law and *love* government, and cling to them, they will be stripped of them.

A treasonous leader can use that powerful apparatus to rule like an autocrat! That is exactly what Barack Obama did. He *said* he was going to "fundamentally transform America"—and that is what he has done. He didn't explain what he meant by that, but now you can see by the fruits what he meant.

THE SOURCE OF POWER

A tyrant who thinks like the devil has gotten control of what is left of the glory and wealth of America. The devil has great power, and he has a burning goal to blot out what God has done and is doing. People who aren't close to God have *no chance* against Satan—and the vast majority of people are quite far from God!

But if you turn to God, He will show you exactly what Satan is doing and give you the power to withstand him.

Satan has the power to conduct great evil and not only hide it but then accuse others of committing it. We saw this with Obama's use of the deep state in general and the Mueller investigation specifically. It is an example of the "depths of Satan" that Jesus Christ warned about (Revelation 2:24). You can prove the real purpose of the Mueller investigation; but Satan knows that if he makes it complicated enough to require deep study to understand it, most people won't dig into it, and he can deceive them. The powerful way Obama works to destroy the nation he was twice elected to lead is one of those "depths."

This is how you can have everyone in power *knowing* that the Mueller investigation was a fraud to cover up what happened surrounding the 2016 election, and *knowing* the fraud surrounding the 2020 election—yet demanding that you say Mueller was completely honest and the 2020 election was completely fair. *They* are like a vile religious cult!

One stunning example was ABC commentator George

Stephanopoulos actually shouting at a Republican senator, *demanding* that he say the election was fair. They *know* that many everyday Americans realize something is wrong. They want to tell you what you can say and even what you can think. And if you don't obey, they will politically, culturally and technologically exile you as they amass more money, influence and power.

YOU MUST RECOGNIZE WHERE THAT ATTITUDE AND THAT SPIRIT COME FROM.

HOW THIS WILL END

With no helper for Israel, many terrible things are going to occur. Already other nations are betraying America, as well as its brother nations Britain and Israel. Iran is developing nuclear weapons. It is seeking ways to humiliate the United States. China is becoming more belligerent. It is targeting U.S. allies like Australia, Hong Kong and Taiwan while drawing closer to America's enemies—holding drills with Iran and backing Cuba. Europe is increasingly determined to become more independent from America and is expanding trade with China. Germany has pursued alignment with Russia through the Nord Stream 2 pipeline and other means. As God prophesied, our national "lovers" are going to betray us and besiege us (Ezekiel 23). America will be left without a single helper!

People are looking to Republicans, to conservative commentators and to preachers for *hope.* The reality is that THERE IS NO HOPE WITHOUT GOD!

Satan is working to blot out the name of Israel. The good news is, God has a master plan to SAVE ISRAEL PERMANENTLY—and He is carrying it out. WITH GOD, THERE IS ENDLESS HOPE.

The world around us is about to die. Bible prophecy shows that it will end in a terribly violent and tragic way. But it will be replaced by a wonderful new world ruled by Jesus Christ. Once that world is here, never again will you hear the words "there was no helper for Israel," because ALL people will *be* Israel and be in the Family of God. What an inspiring hope!

CHAPTER EIGHT

STOLEN ELECTION, FAKE INSURRECTION

I N AN OCTOBER 2020 INTERVIEW, JOE BIDEN SAID, "WE HAVE PUT together ... the most extensive and inclusive voter fraud organization in the history of American politics." He obviously did not intend to say that, but it is hard to ignore when *extensive, organized voter fraud* is precisely what brought him to power.

It is practically an open secret that radical Democrats stole the 2020 United States presidential election. One month after the election, a Quinnipiac University poll of 978 registered voters nationwide found that 77 percent of Republicans believed there was widespread voter fraud during the election, and 34 percent of all registered voters thought Biden's win was illegitimate. And the share of Americans who view Joe Biden as a fake president has only gone up since. An Axios poll of 2,649 registered voters taken in January 2022 found that more than 40 percent of Americans do not believe Biden legitimately won the election. That indicates OVER 100 MILLION AMERICANS BELIEVE THE ELECTION WAS STOLEN, including a lot of Democrats. In fact, many Democrats *know* it was stolen.

Official totals show a record 74.2 million people voted for President Donald Trump—nearly 5 million more than any candidate in American history. Yet somehow, Joe Biden officially received *7 million more votes than that.* He won 12 million more votes than Barack Obama did.

This official total was not reached because of an unprecedented swell of enthusiasm for a singularly capable and attractive presidential candidate. Joe Biden was a 47-year career politician prone to gaffes and linked to corruption, who mostly campaigned from his basement. Biden's vote count was reached by careful planning, blatant lawlessness, rank corruption, shameless deceit and pervasive propaganda.

Information on the extent of the voter fraud is copious. One of the better sources is the third volume of Dr. Peter Navarro's study on electoral fraud. It uncovered 3,069,002 "possible illegal votes" in just the swing states of Arizona, Georgia, Michigan, Nevada, Pennsylvania and Wisconsin. Since Joe Biden's "victory" margin in all of these states *combined* was a 10th of that (312,992 votes), no reasonable person can conclude the presidential election was free and fair, much less "the most secure election in American history," as leftists in politics and the media keep insisting.

Yet America's justice system refused to investigate voter fraud. The Trump administration filed at least 63 lawsuits alleging fraud in several states. Almost all of these suits were thrown out—not on the merits, but over technicalities.

As a number of reports, statistical analyses, documentaries and other sources have established, the 2020 presidential election was plagued by voter fraud. It was organized. It was extensive. It was extreme, defiant and flagrant. And there was someone behind it who had the power, motive and gall to commit the greatest electoral steal in history. It was not Joe Biden, but he knows exactly who it was.

What was worth committing such treason for?

The main goal was to restore to power the political machinery of Barack Obama. He and his operatives worked furiously during the Trump presidency, during his reelection bid, and especially during the election itself.

PULLING STRINGS

Barack Obama was the first president in more than a century to stay in Washington, D.C., after leaving office. All other presidents left the capital out of respect for their successor, the presidency and the nation. Why did Obama remain? In March 2017, Britain's *Daily Mail* wrote that Obama's home, just a few miles from the White House, had become the "nerve center of the mounting insurgency against his successor, President Donald J. Trump."

This British paper could recognize exactly what was happening: Headquartered in D.C., this man was commanding the radical left the entire time. Mr. Obama was personally involved in seeking to overthrow President Trump! *Insurgency* is the right word.

In March 2020, Obama guided the selection of Joe Biden as the Democratic presidential nominee. For example, he directly called Pete Buttigieg after he pulled out of the race and asked him to endorse Biden. His aides made similar calls to candidates Amy Klobuchar and Elizabeth Warren.

Between March and November, Obama and his team campaigned hard for Joe Biden. Biden's vice president, Kamala Harris, was also hand-selected by Mr. Obama.

Barack Obama kept his name out of most of the headlines, but he was exerting his power constantly. His destructive leadership is unparalleled in U.S. history! The only reason more people cannot recognize this is that Satan's deception in the world has reached unprecedented intensity. Most people cannot see the spiritual dimension of this crisis *at all.*

These radicals pushed for major and unconstitutional changes to election laws, and they implemented election procedures that outright violated existing laws. They used electronic voting systems with poor security. They demanded massive expansion of the use of obviously fraud-prone mail-in ballots. We now know that much of the fraud was committed with these mail-in votes. To take just one example, undercover journalist organization Project Veritas discovered *thousands* of registered voters in Georgia who all shared a single address across the street from Georgia Secretary of State Brad Raffensperger's office at the state capitol.

By November 3, the radical left was ready to manipulate an election.

ELECTION DAY

As the left-wing media had predicted and planned for, on Election Day Donald Trump got off to a huge lead, taking crucial swing states Florida and Ohio. Rarely do candidates lose when they win those two states. *Time* later published an article by Molly Ball titled "The Secret History of the Shadow Campaign That Saved the 2020 Election." Ball explained Democrats' reaction to Trump's massive lead: "Election Night began with many Democrats despairing. Trump was running ahead of preelection polling, winning Florida, Ohio and Texas easily and keeping Michigan, Wisconsin and Pennsylvania too close to call" (Feb. 4, 2021).

Ball explained that Democratic leaders and left-wing activists joined a video call together at 11 p.m. that evening to discuss what to do. Activists were standing by, ready to take to the streets if the election didn't swing in Biden's favor.

Then, at 11:20, Fox News decided to call Arizona for Biden while a large portion of the vote was still out, especially in Republican-leaning Maricopa County. Meanwhile, Fox refused to call states like Ohio and Florida, where Donald Trump was ahead by large margins and a higher percentage of the vote was in. Arizona would be the first state to "flip" in the 2020 election, and this proved to be the beginning of a momentum shift.

Many people went to bed the night of November 3 thinking Donald Trump had won the election handily, only to wake up the next morning to see swing states like Pennsylvania, Wisconsin, Michigan and Georgia flip to Joe Biden.

What happened over the next few days was unlike anything America had ever seen. Stunningly, Democrats had been "warning" people for months to expect exactly what happened. How did they know?

In Fulton County, Georgia, the state's largest and most corrupt county, mail-in ballots were counted at the State Farm arena. On the evening of November 3, officials at the arena said they were finished counting ballots for the night and that poll watchers and the media needed to leave. But a few poll workers stayed behind and—illegally—continued counting ballots without poll watchers present. Video footage showed poll workers running ballots through counting machines multiple times. A corresponding spike in Biden votes put him even with President Trump. Over the following days, Democrats managed to produce enough ballots to give Biden the victory by about 11,000 votes.

In Pennsylvania, President Trump watched a 600,000-vote lead evaporate overnight. In Pittsburgh, poll workers were told to stop counting and return in the morning. In Philadelphia, heavily Democratic precincts would not allow Republican poll watchers to observe the counting process in defiance of court orders. Democrats control the state's supreme court and the executive office, so it is difficult to uncover any wrongdoing.

In Detroit, Michigan, like in Fulton County, mail-in ballots were all processed at one central location, the TCF Center. Surveillance footage showed a white van pulling into the facility in the early morning hours, long after the deadline had passed for ballots to be submitted. Men unloaded boxes of mail-in ballots from the van. Attorney General Barr later said he looked into the matter and was told this was just how elections in Detroit are handled. Really? As tensions rose at the TCF Center over the following days, poll watchers and the media were prohibited from observing the counting process. Poll workers put up cardboard to cover windows where counting was taking place.

Similarly in Milwaukee, Wisconsin, mail-in ballots were delivered to the counting center in the middle of the night. Each time the mail-in ballots were counted, Trump's lead would disappear. In Green Bay, Wisconsin, Democrats actually had keys to the ballot storage rooms! This is because the city was given a million-dollar grant by a Democratic nonprofit that made the money conditional on their chosen people being able to run parts of the election process in cities like Green Bay. That same nonprofit gave a disproportionate amount of money to Democratic strongholds in swing states.

These are just a few of the alarming, unprecedented events that took place on Election Night.

There is also the statistical data showing how unusual Biden's so-called victory really was, including his losing 18 of the 19 "bellwether counties" and underperforming in Democratic areas outside of the swing states.

In addition, a great deal of suspicious and lawless behavior suggests Democrats are running perhaps the greatest cover-up in American history. Democrats threatened violence to prevent Republicans from investigating the election. In Michigan, Democrats threatened the children of county officials who said they would refuse to certify the election because there were so many irregularities. In Maricopa County, Arizona, county officials refused to hand over hard drives with 2020 election information to auditors in defiance of a court order. In Georgia, video footage shows people depositing multiple ballots into drop boxes in violation of state laws. Filmmaker Dinesh D'Souza produced a documentary in 2022 titled *2000 Mules* exposing the Democrats' strategy of stuffing drop boxes with mail-in ballots.

All this was covered up by media outlets. They were complicit in the fraud! On Election Day, the *New York Times* tweeted, "The role of declaring the winner of a presidential election in the U.S. falls to the news media." It quickly retracted that post, but that says all you need to know about how they think.

On November 7, 2020, despite all the irregularities and evidence of crimes, leftist news corporations, in coordination, declared Joe Biden America's next president.

'JOEBAMA'

When Biden and Harris nominated and appointed individuals for executive offices in the new administration, many of these people were either close to Obama or had been part of his administration. In a November 23, 2020, interview with *Politico,* Mr. Obama was pleased. "You're seeing a team develop that I have great confidence in," he said. Of course he had great confidence in them: They were HIS PEOPLE! OBAMA EVEN ADMITTED THAT 90 PERCENT OF BIDEN'S CABINET WAS COMPOSED OF HIS PEOPLE.

In the *Epoch Times,* Lee Smith wrote, "Obama wants it understood that Biden is an avatar for a third Obama term. Now he can complete the work of 'fundamentally transforming America,' as he put it days before the 2008 election" (Nov. 17, 2020).

Freddy Gray, editor of *Spectator USA,* used the term *Joebama* to describe the incoming presidency. "Obama sounds a bit of a World King these days, but you can't blame him for feeling chipper. ... [H]is great nemesis Donald Trump appears finally to have been vanquished—and his gang is taking charge of Washington again. ... In fact, the incoming Biden administration is arguably *more Obamaish than the original Obama administration was"* (Nov. 28, 2020). One Biden campaign staff member even told *Politico,* "The Obama staffers are now cutting out the people who got Biden elected."

BY MID-DECEMBER, WHAT AMOUNTED TO A THIRD OBAMA ADMINISTRATION WAS READY TO MOVE BACK INTO THE WHITE HOUSE.

The most remarkable part was, most Americans had no problem with this. Obama's presence in Biden's election campaign, victory and appointments never received the scrutiny it deserved. To most people—especially the mainstream media, which swoons over Obama—it was a *positive* factor. But prophetically, it is a huge concern. ANTIOCHUS WAS ILLEGALLY, TREASONOUSLY, TAKING BACK CONTROL, AND MOST AMERICANS DIDN'T SEEM TO CARE. Obama's plan was to end up back in the White House—at the very least as the puppet master directing Joe Biden and Kamala Harris—to pursue his great goal to fundamentally transform America.

Obama himself said this in an interview with comedian Stephen Colbert in November 2020: "People would ask me, knowing what you know now, do you wish you had a third term? And I used to say, if I could make an arrangement where I had a stand-in, a front man or a front woman, and they had an earpiece in, and I was just in my basement in my sweats looking through the stuff, and I could sort of deliver the lines but somebody else was doing all the talking and ceremony, I would be fine with that because I found the work fascinating." Mr. Obama has made other similar statements indicating his desire to wield power.

Jesus said, "[O]ut of the abundance of the heart the mouth speaketh" (Matthew 12:34).

The 2020 election steal put this man very much back in control, ready to rule through an illegitimate president.

AN EFFORT TO OBTAIN JUSTICE

In the weeks after the election, one legal challenge after another was ignored, denied or defeated, even by the Supreme Court. Then, two weeks before the inauguration, Congress met to certify the election results on January 6, 2021.

A "Save America" rally of about 200,000 people gathered in Washington to protest the election fraud and theft. President Trump addressed the crowd and said he knew the attendees would march to the Capitol to "peacefully and patriotically" make their voices heard.

Crowds did make their way to the Capitol. Videos show police spraying tear gas on people who were protesting peacefully. Some people began to clash with police. Despite Democrats' efforts to suppress key security footage, plenty of video and eyewitness accounts reveal that the Capitol was lightly guarded, "restricted area" signs were moved early on, and police admitted protesters into the building. They were trying to incite the crowd. Some protesters smashed windows, some vandalized Speaker of the House Nancy Pelosi's office, and some entered the Senate Chamber. Others in the crowd tried to stop the vandals and trespassers and pleaded with police to do more to stop them. Members of Congress evacuated for a few hours as police resecured the building.

The protesters killed no one, and not one used a gun. The only shooting victim was Ashli Babbitt, an unarmed protester who presented no danger at all but was shot and killed by a Capitol Police officer. When the blood flows like that, it becomes more sobering.

This was an ugly day in American history. People who committed wrongs such as vandalizing that great historic building should be reprimanded appropriately. After the Capitol was breached, President Trump himself told protesters to maintain law and order, to support law enforcement, and to "go home now." He later urged "no violence, no lawbreaking and no vandalism of any kind."

But radical elites in government and media seized on this unruly protest. They took an incident involving people who committed misdemeanor trespassing to protest a treasonous election and called it an assault on American democracy worse than Pearl Harbor, 9/11, or anything else since the Civil War. They branded it an INSURRECTION and used it to target their political enemies for censoring, smearing, silencing, boycotting, prosecuting, imprisoning and worse. They used it as a weapon to utterly destroy their opposition.

It has become one of the most chilling examples of the attack on America.

ROSENBERG'S ADMISSION

On March 8–9, 2022, two important videos were published that were largely overlooked. They were produced by Project Veritas, which investigates and exposes corruption and fraud, often by tricking people into divulging information and secretly recording them. These two videos show Pulitzer Prize-winning journalist Matthew Rosenberg in a conversation about his employer, the *New York Times.*

Rosenberg is a national security correspondent. He was outside the U.S. Capitol on January 6 with two other colleagues, "and we were just having fun," he said. He also said, "I know I'm supposed to be traumatized," and he mocked other journalists who "keep going on about their trauma" over being at the Capitol that day. He said they were "not in any danger" and were misrepresenting the situation. He said the crowd was not organized and that "[T]HERE WERE A TON OF FBI INFORMANTS AMONG THE PEOPLE WHO ATTACKED THE CAPITOL."

Rosenberg was admitting the truth and contradicting what the *New York Times* had been saying for more than a year: The protest on January 6, 2021, was not an organized insurrection by Trump supporters.

But radicals in politics and the media acted as if everyone had been traumatized. On January 7, Pelosi ordered a fence erected around the Capitol and brought in the National Guard, keeping troops there for months. People arrested for trespassing, who might not have even known they were trespassing, have been treated like terrorists, held in jail for months without trial. They were not executing an insurrection on January 6; they were *protesting* the insurrection of November 3!

Rosenberg is no conservative. But as he pointed out some comparatively minor wrongs committed on that day, he said, "[T]he left's overreaction ... to it, in some places, was so over the top." Yes, there were wrongs committed, but they were very minor compared to an *insurrection.* And many or most of them were instigated by leftists who infiltrated the protest *to create trouble!*

WHAT WAS THE FBI DOING THERE?

It has emerged that RADICAL-LEFTIST ACTIVISTS INCLUDING ANTIFA AND BLACK LIVES MATTER HAD INFILTRATED THE CROWD, pretending to be Trump supporters and trying to cause Antifa-style violence.

JOHN SULLIVAN, A WELL-KNOWN LEFTIST AGITATOR WHO FOUNDED A GROUP NAMED INSURGENCE USA, IS SEEN IN VIDEO FOOTAGE WEARING A TRUMP HAT OUTSIDE THE BUILDING AND ATTEMPTING TO INCITE THE CROWD TO ANGER. He was also recorded inside at the scene of the fatal shooting. He is one of the individuals who smashed the window in the Speaker's Lobby while officers on the other side had their weapons drawn. This was the window that Ashli Babbitt then tried to climb through when she was shot. When the officer pulled the trigger and she fell to the floor bleeding from the neck, Sullivan was within feet of her, recording video. He reportedly began claiming she was dead, though this probably was not the case at the time and police who were immediately on the scene said they could save her. Even as blood was spilled, Sullivan was trying to whip up the crowd and make a bad situation worse. Later that day, Sullivan went on camera, including at CNN, to give his account of the violence inside the Capitol. The interviewers did not question what he, a leftist agitator, was doing there.

More and more evidence is emerging that deep state agents *wanted* people like Sullivan to cause trouble and that leftist media were eager to portray this as something it wasn't.

For example, among the January 6 crowd were numerous FBI informants. Footage from before the protest shows one man, Ray Epps, directly inciting protesters to go inside the Capitol. The crowd around him yelled, "No!" and began chanting, "Fed!" They recognized that their own government was trying to turn their protest violent. IT HAS SINCE BEEN REVEALED THAT THERE WERE ABOUT 100 FBI AGITATORS IN THAT CROWD!

WHY? This is deeply disturbing. What were they trying to accomplish? How many of the instigators were people working with the FBI?

When Fox News reported on those Rosenberg videos, it covered the fact that he said the danger that day was drastically exaggerated, but IT DID NOT EVEN DISCUSS HIS COMMENT THAT "THERE WERE A TON OF FBI INFORMANTS." It appears network executives instructed their journalists not to discuss that. That is at Fox News, which is supposed to be conservative. The *New York Times* and America's other largest news organizations are much more radically liberal. And the executives there are very focused on shaping the narrative surrounding January 6 for an important, specific reason.

WHO GAINED FROM JANUARY 6?

Inside the Capitol on January 6, 2021, MORE THAN 100 MEMBERS OF CONGRESS WERE READY TO OPPOSE THE CERTIFICATION OF THE 2020 PRESIDENTIAL ELECTION. People in six battleground states had been crying out about significant voter fraud that had occurred. Radicals had committed a massive treasonous act to steal the election, and in some important ways, they had been *caught!* A great deal of fraud had been uncovered; huge numbers of votes had been stolen in six states. THOSE 100-PLUS LEGISLATORS WERE READY TO ADDRESS THE ELECTION CRIMES that had given Joe Biden an inconceivable 81 million votes. These members of Congress were ready to STAND UP FOR THE TRUTH AND TRY TO STOP A STOLEN ELECTION.

BUT THE JANUARY 6 PROTEST, AND THE LEFT'S REACTION TO IT, CHANGED ALL THAT.

"... Donald Trump had nothing to gain and everything to lose by the violent assault on the Capitol that day," Frank Miele wrote for RealClearPolitics. "The only chance of keeping Trump in the White House was not by invading the Capitol, but by keeping it secure while our representatives debated the validity of the election using the entirely constitutional process taking place inside the halls of Congress" (Jan. 3, 2022). That is a critical truth! DONALD TRUMP HAD NOTHING AT ALL TO GAIN FROM AN ASSAULT ON THE CAPITOL THAT DAY.

"The electoral votes of at least five states were being challenged—not in a coup, but in a lawful manner also used by Democrats in earlier elections," Miele continued. Think of the 2000 presidential election between Al Gore and George W. Bush, which came down to certifying the vote in Florida. Gore claimed there was fraud, so Democrats pushed hard for every legal challenge possible to dispute the vote there. But they have shown that they think such recourse is only for Democrats, not Republicans.

On January 6, 2021, "Republican senators and House members had lined up to make the case to the public and their fellow constitutional officers that something was rotten in the states of Arizona, Georgia, Pennsylvania, Wisconsin and Michigan, and that the election was therefore tainted," Miele wrote. Everything they sought to do was according to the Constitution. *"But the violence outside resulted in a sharply truncated debate inside* that was virtually ignored, if not outright mocked or shamed, by the mainstream media. THE RIOT INSTANTLY DOOMED ANY CHANCE TRUMP HAD OF PREVAILING IN HIS ARGUMENT THAT THE ELECTION WAS STOLEN" (ibid).

That is the point: Trump had nothing to gain from that violence, but THE RADICAL LEFT HAD EVERYTHING TO GAIN! The January 6 event ENDED EVERYTHING FOR PRESIDENT TRUMP. ALMOST NOBODY STOOD UP FOR HIM, FOR THE CONSTITUTION OR FOR AMERICA.

Rosenberg seems to think the radical left's "over the top" reaction to the "insurrection" is unfortunate for less radical leftists. He does not realize that *the over-the-top reaction was the point.* To *cover up* their stolen election and certify their treasonous coup, the radicals had to commit MORE TREASON. That is why the January 6 protest included "a ton" of FBI informants, and also radical leftists and even FBI agitators: THEY WANTED TO USE THAT PROTEST TO COVER THEIR TREASON. Radicals stole the 2020 election—*then* instigated the uglier aspects of January 6—*then* overreacted to that protest to discredit it AND TO BLOCK ALL OPPOSITION TO CERTIFYING THE STOLEN ELECTION.

Their plan worked perfectly: *Those 100 members of Congress and the vice president caved in.*

A LACK OF COURAGE

In the speech President Trump gave that day, he made a direct appeal to his vice president, who had a role in certifying the election. "Mike Pence, I hope you're going to stand up for the good of our Constitution, and for the good of our country," he said. "And if you're not, I'm going to be very disappointed in you. I'm going to tell you right now, I'm not hearing good stories."

After Mr. Pence allowed the fraudulent vote to be certified,

President Trump posted on social media: "Mike Pence didn't have the courage to do what should have been done to protect our country and our Constitution, giving states a chance to certify, correct a set of facts, not the fraudulent and inaccurate ones, which they were asked to previously certify."

What kind of treachery is that? Would state legislatures continue to fight for the president when even the vice president won't? Constitutionally, Mr. Pence could have and should have *demanded* an investigation. But he said: "It is my considered judgment that my oath to support and defend the Constitution constrains me from claiming unilateral authority to determine which electoral votes should be counted, and which should not."

That was a twisted lie. He was not "supporting and defending the Constitution" by ignoring people in six swing states crying out about fraud everywhere! Criminals had *trampled all over* the Constitution! Nobody was asking Mr. Pence to change votes: They were asking for lawful protection from *stolen* votes.

"Pence had the authority as the [vice president] not to certify," former Trump official Peter Navarro told the *Daily Mail* (Nov. 1, 2021). He explained that those 100-plus members of Congress were prepared "to call into question the results in the six battleground states, which would yield us 12 hours of televised hearings about all the election irregularities." These hearings could have "galvanized the American public behind the reality that this election is likely stolen, and all Pence had to do was say there's enough uncertainty here that we need to send this back to the states and to look at this and then we'll come back in two weeks and make the decision. That's all he had to do," Navarro said.

But the violence brought this plan to an abrupt halt. Republican leaders Mitch McConnell and Kevin McCarthy used "the excuse of the violence on Capitol Hill to halt any further attempt to challenge the election results," Navarro said.

That is *precisely* why the radical leftists *wanted* chaos at the Capitol on that day.

"... Michael Richard Pence will have secured his place in

history as the Brutus most responsible both for the final betrayal of President Trump and the unceremonious burial of election integrity," Navarro said.

These Republican leaders betrayed the president. And the courts, all the way up to the Supreme Court, threw out the legal challenges due to technicalities. They all ran, like Jonah, from their duty.

And because Republicans caved, Joe Biden was inaugurated.

The very afternoon after being sworn in, Joe Biden signed 17 executive orders aimed mainly at destroying what President Trump had done for the American economy, energy, border and education. He has gone on to advance Obama's agenda of blotting out America's history, traditions and biblical foundations; allowing immigrants, including criminals and drug smugglers, to pour over the border; spending billions on housing, health care, education and welfare; and sinking this country into $30 trillion in debt. This is plunging the nation into an unprecedented radicalized future.

IMPEACHMENT

It takes extreme measures to steal and keep power. But that is what radical leftists, including those in Washington, resorted to.

On January 13, 2021, just one week before Donald Trump's presidential term expired, the House of Representatives *impeached* him for his speech on January 6. It was the fastest impeachment in history—and the second impeachment of this president, just 56 weeks after the first. They accused him of "incitement of insurrection," charging him for "willfully inciting violence against the government of the United States."

It was a ridiculous charge. Even liberal law professor Jonathan Turley noted that President Trump "never actually called for violence or a riot." In fact, President Trump had asked for 10,000 National Guardsmen to keep order on January 6. But Pelosi, who is partially in charge of Capitol security, said no, as did the Capitol Police and the mayor of Washington, D.C. (*After* January 6, however, Pelosi and others called in the Guard and erected a fence as though the area were a high-danger zone.)

Pelosi admitted that this impeachment was partly an attempt to eliminate any chance of Trump holding public office in the future.

Joe Biden was then inaugurated, and Mr. Trump left town. The impeachment case was brought to the Senate, but they failed to reach the necessary two-thirds majority, so the president was acquitted. Still, every Democrat and *seven Republican senators* voted to convict Mr. Trump. Some Republicans dislike the way President Trump disrupted the political status quo; they want to purge the party of his influence. All these efforts are far more destructive to America than most people realize!

Meanwhile, media and technology executives colluded to use the January 6 riot as a pretext to muzzle Donald Trump. Twitter suspended him that very day. The next day, January 7, former First Lady Michelle Obama wrote an open letter telling tech companies to "stop enabling this monstrous behavior." In less than 24 hours, the bans started. Twitter banned Mr. Trump permanently so his 88 million Twitter followers could no longer read his messages.* Facebook shut down his account. Apple, Discord, Google, Instagram, Pinterest, Reddit, Shopify, Snapchat, Stripe, TikTok, Twitch, YouTube and other major platforms banned or restricted his messages and those of his followers in some form. These great high-tech corporations acted like they were too "righteous" to allow people to read or hear what the president said, when their outlets are full of filth and sewage! Major television networks refused to broadcast the farewell speech of the president of the United States. The political director at ABC News said authorities must begin "cleansing the movement" associated with President Trump.

The federal government was already starting its "cleansing."

---

* For perspective, Biden had 20 million Twitter followers; and half of those were later discovered to be fake.

PATRIOT PURGE

The FBI launched a nationwide campaign to get people to report those who attended the January 6 protest. The government arrested and jailed Trump supporters for months without giving them a day in court. They won't address the evidence of radical instigators, federal informants and even federal instigators hijacking a peaceful protest; federal charging documents include a number of unnamed, unindicted coconspirators. (According to Revolver News, the reason some protesters haven't been indicted is that they are FBI agitators or actual agents.) But they will proclaim that this bunch of tourists was committing "insurrection."

These were the same people who portrayed the 2020 Black Lives Matter protests in which buildings were burned and people died as "mostly peaceful"!

In February 2023, the incoming Republican House Speaker, Kevin McCarthy, gave Fox News host Tucker Carlson access to the 14,000 hours of footage that were recorded at the January 6 event. The bits that Carlson broadcast made even plainer what was already painfully clear: that the "insurrection" was fake, that the vast majority of the people there were peacefully protesting, and that the way radicals are using that event as a political weapon is diabolical!

One couple was at the Capitol and saw the protest but never went inside the building. They sensed something was not right. After returning home to Alaska, one day, FBI agents knocked on their door. They claimed they were looking for Nancy Pelosi's laptop, took over their home, confiscated the couple's pocket copy of the U.S. Constitution, and handcuffed both of them.

THE GOVERNMENT STILL HAS MANY PEOPLE IN JAIL WHO HAVE NEVER BEEN TRIED—SOME OF THEM IN SOLITARY CONFINEMENT. WE EXPECT THIS IN DICTATORSHIPS LIKE RUSSIA OR CHINA—BUT AMERICA?

Biden's regime has repeatedly claimed that "terrorism from white supremacy is the most lethal threat to the homeland today" and has attacked patriotism and constitutional principles as "racist" and worse, even within the U.S. military. The regime is monitoring the online activity of military personnel for "extremist behavior." The effort is led by a man who has said that only racists, misogynists and extremists support Donald Trump. One senator introduced legislation to classify "Make America Great Again" rallies as "domestic terrorist activity." Even parents upset with school boards indoctrinating their children in sexual perversion are being targeted!

In a good government, the authorities must protect the people most of all. But the American government is not protecting Americans—it is, in fact, purging the patriots! These elites are committing crimes and treason and treating everyday Americans like criminals and traitors!

We are getting a good look at what 21st-century authoritarianism looks like. And it is being driven by former Obama administration agents led, behind the scenes, by Barack Obama.

JONAH

Look again at the prophecy in 2 Kings 14. Verses 23 and 25 say, "In the fifteenth year of Amaziah the son of Joash king of Judah Jeroboam the son of Joash king of Israel began to reign in Samaria, and reigned forty and one years. ... He restored the coast of Israel from the entering of Hamath unto the sea of the plain, according to the word of the LORD God of Israel, *which he spake by the hand of his servant Jonah,* the son of Amittai, the prophet, which was of Gathhepher."

The Prophet Jonah prophesied that Jeroboam would intervene and save the kingdom of Israel. This shows that God had a prophet on the scene during this crucial period in Israel's history. God was there, and so was His prophet, letting everybody know that He was involved and that He would not let the name of Israel be blotted out!

The reference to Jonah in 2 Kings 14:25 is encouraging. God wants us to know, amid all these grave events and fulfilled prophecies, that He is here, sending out His prophetic message, and directing events according to His purposes!

There is also a message in the fact that it was *Jonah* who gave this prophecy. This is the same Jonah whom God later commissioned to warn Nineveh, that "exceeding great city," the capital of the Assyrian Empire (Jonah 1:2; 3:3). God wanted Jonah to tell the leaders of that mighty and cruel empire that He was about to punish them for their evil.

Jonah feared doing that, and he fled. By running away, he committed a serious sin before God.

This history teaches a crucial lesson: We must not run from anything God wants us to do. Of course there are things we would rather not do, but we *must do* what God asks of us, no matter how difficult. When facing difficulties, we must be tough and brace ourselves to the task.

Jonah ran from his duty at first. Republicans have abandoned their duty. God has a message for America today, and I must not run from this duty—I have an obligation before God to deliver it.

Jonah was punished by being swallowed by a great fish for three days and three nights. He then repented and went right into Nineveh, proclaiming to them that burdensome message (Jonah 3). Then something astonishing happened: The leaders and people of Nineveh *believed God.* The people of this great city and mighty empire humbled themselves (verses 5-10).

This really happened! These ancestors of the modern Germans, from the king to the nobles to all the people, repented! THAT IS THE ONLY TIME AN EMPIRE HAS EVER REPENTED AT THE WARNING OF A PROPHET OF GOD.

I'm sure God wants this history emphasized. God *deeply desires* for people to repent. Even in America today, as acute as the problems destroying our country are, we could turn everything around if we, like the Ninevites, would humble ourselves before God and repent.

CHAPTER NINE

THIS IS NOT INCOMPETENCE

D URING THE FIRST YEAR OF HIS FAKE PRESIDENCY, IN 2021, Joe Biden announced that America would end its war in Afghanistan unconditionally and at all costs.

Our nation lost nearly 2,500 troops and spent $275 million per day every day for 7,267 days on the war in Afghanistan—more than $2 trillion in 20 years. Yet our soldiers were evacuated in absurd haste to leave that nation to barbarians. THE MIGHTY AMERICAN MILITARY SIMPLY *SURRENDERED* TO THE TALIBAN.

It was an abject, shameful dishonor for America—THE WORST FOREIGN-POLICY DISASTER IN THE NATION'S HISTORY. This terrible defeat was a spectacle seen by the entire world—and they were watching intently! It will mar our history for the rest of time.

The Taliban, a primitive organization of around 75,000 fighters, threatened America—the most overwhelmingly powerful nation in history—that if it didn't completely vacate by the end of August 2021, it would face consequences. Many other nations with people in Afghanistan pleaded with Joe Biden to remain and get everyone out no matter how long it took. Biden refused. *He obeyed his orders from the Taliban!*

Joe Biden is commander in chief of the most militarily sophisticated nation in world history. He could have used that power to drive the Taliban and every other terrorist group out of Kabul for as long as he wanted!

But he didn't. Instead he *begged* the Taliban to let our people out. He OBEYED THEM—even though doing so meant enraging and alienating America's allies, abandoning American citizens, and humiliating America.

With its rushed pullout, the Biden administration catastrophically squandered 20 years of sacrifices in Afghanistan in mere days. It permitted the very extremist group we went in to destroy to regain control and revive a radical Islamist state. Before evacuating, it abandoned a massive air base that would have made a withdrawal far easier and safer. It left 5,000 terrorists in its prison that the Taliban were able to set free. It left behind hundreds of Americans and abandoned thousands of Afghan allies. It sent an unmistakable message to both allies and enemies worldwide: *America does not keep its promises. We do not honor commitments. We cannot be trusted even to protect our own people!*

Life in Afghanistan quickly returned to nightmarish Taliban rule: people being persecuted and killed; girls age 15 and even younger being rounded up and given to Taliban fighters as "wives"; women being publicly executed for failing to wear a burka; children and women being abused, raped and murdered.

Usually when America retreats from a war zone, if it has to leave any armaments behind it destroys them so they won't fall into enemy hands. The Biden administration did the opposite. It gave a staggering $85 BILLION worth of U.S. military equipment to this extremist group—including that massive air base, 2,000 armored vehicles, 45 Black Hawk helicopters, 208 total aircraft, 10,000 air-to-ground rockets, over 2,500 bombs, and millions of U.S. dollars in cash. Victor Davis Hanson noted that the night-vision equipment, more than 20,000 grenades and 1,400 grenade launchers, more than 7,000 machine guns and 600,000 small arms, and millions of rounds of ammunition are "the perfect equipment for jihadist terror operations and asymmetrical street fighting" (Independent Institute, Aug. 30, 2021). OVERNIGHT, AMERICA CREATED ONE OF THE MOST WELL-FUNDED, HEAVILY ARMED TERRORIST NATIONS IN THE WORLD.

Hanson compared this haul of armaments with the military aid America has given to Israel over the last 70 years, which has totaled around $100 billion. "In other words, in one fell SWOOP, THE PENTAGON DEPOSITED INTO TALIBAN HANDS ABOUT 80 PERCENT OF ALL THE MILITARY AID THAT WE'VE EVER GIVEN TO ISRAEL SINCE THE FOUNDING OF THE JEWISH STATE" (ibid).

WHAT A WRETCHED DEED BY THE AMERICAN "SUPERPOWER"! This is as shameful as anything America has ever done. This disaster was the *worst evidence ever* of how the United States has COLLAPSED as a superpower! Other nations around the world see this clearly. They are taking advantage of this and preparing to replace American dominance with their own.

Many people said this catastrophe proved Joe Biden's incompetence. But it wasn't the result of bungling and bad judgment. IT WAS PART OF A DELIBERATE, PLANNED EFFORT TO DESTROY AMERICA. And it was terribly successful.

The facts are irrefutable. Many people see the damage President Biden is doing. The most clear-eyed analysts recognize the horrible likelihood that THERE MUST BE MALICIOUS INTENT BEHIND IT. Former war correspondent Lara Logan told Fox News that this administration wants you to believe "that Afghanistan is complicated," but in reality, "the United States *wants* this outcome." She said America's leaders "could do anything they want to change this. And they're not" (Aug. 18, 2021).

She is absolutely right. These actions truly cannot be explained any other way. This wasn't simply the result of ineptitude on the part of this administration or naivety about how the world really works. These were the aftereffects of a calculated, aggressive, satanic attack aimed at weakening and ultimately destroying the nations of Israel, starting with the world's most powerful nation.

This was evidenced in the way all the civilian and military leaders in Joe Biden's administration called the evacuation a tremendous *success!* They repeatedly said that everything went according to plan, and that it was a "heroic and historic" operation. Reporters pressed them on whether they felt they made any mistakes, and the answer—time and again—was NO! This proves just how arrogant and impervious to correction these leaders are. But even more—it shows you that THEY PLANNED for this operation to be so disastrous. It all followed their plan—to America's great hurt.

THIS IS ANTIOCHUS-THINKING. It is "blot out the name of Israel" thinking. It is inspired by the devil working to bring down America. This has become so plain that *anybody* ought to be able to understand him and the crises he is causing.

THE OBAMA YEARS

When America announced it would leave Afghanistan by August 31, 2021, the Taliban began taking over the country at lightning pace. Sources said the offensive was masterminded by Khairullah Khairkhwa, a jihadist who had long aimed to eliminate America's presence from Afghanistan. He promised Biden's White House that if the U.S. removed all its troops, the Taliban wouldn't attack. He became the chief Taliban negotiator dealing with the Biden administration.

The fact that Biden's team would talk with this man is deeply condemning. It turns out, America knew him well. He had been captured and was confined at Guantanamo Bay. "Mullah Khairkhwa previously served as the Taliban's interior minister in Afghanistan, where he oversaw enforcement of brutal Islamist punishments, including beheadings and stonings," the *New York Post* reported. "After 9/11, he was arrested in Pakistan and sent to Gitmo in 2002. The Pentagon accused him of closely associating with Osama bin Laden and bin Laden's al Qaeda henchmen" (Aug. 16, 2021). Khairkhwa and four other high-ranking Taliban terrorists were to be lifetime prisoners there. The Pentagon called them the "hardest of the hard core" among Guantanamo prisoners.

BUT THESE FIVE MEN WERE RELEASED—BY BARACK OBAMA. HE LET THEM GO IN 2014 IN EXCHANGE FOR U.S. ARMY DESERTER BOWE BERGDAHL.

This move proved to be deadly. As soon as Khairkhwa was

released, he went back to his terrorist activities. And in the Afghanistan pullout, he helped deal a crushing blow to America!

Still, Mr. Obama—through the Biden administration—*treated this man as a trustworthy negotiation partner.* This is TREASONOUS!

IT ALSO DIRECTLY LINKED THE DISASTER IN AFGHANISTAN WITH BARACK OBAMA.

Most people only look at the surface. All the blame and anger over the Afghanistan fiasco was directed at Joe Biden. People failed to see the bigger picture. I believe Barack Obama *intended* Biden to take the flak for what happened. It all fulfilled his desires perfectly: America retreated and proved itself to be a spent power; Islamists took control of Afghanistan and became ascendant in the Middle East. Joe Biden took the fall for all of it. And Obama was free to continue his work.

This is just *one example* of how so many of the seeds for the Afghanistan disaster were laid when Biden was *vice* president, and the president was Barack Obama.

For eight years, Obama pursued treacherous anti-American, anti-Israel, pro-Iran, pro-Muslim policies. In Egypt, after that nation had peace with Israel for 30 years, Obama helped kick Hosni Mubarak out of power in favor of the Muslim Brotherhood, and he would not speak out against Mohamed Morsi essentially declaring himself pharaoh of Egypt and a bitter enemy of the Jewish nation. Obama allowed an American outpost in Benghazi, Libya, to be overrun by jihadis, and a U.S. ambassador and three other Americans were killed waiting for help that never arrived; yet Obama didn't consider this any cause for concern. He failed to enforce his own demands on Syria, with its witch's brew of weapons of mass destruction, undermining America's strength and leaving a murderous dictator in place.

Most importantly, he empowered the most extreme elements within the world's number one terrorist nation, Iran. In 2011, he turned his back on the people of Iran who rose up in protest against their tyrannical leaders. And as that regime withered under economic sanctions, Obama threw it a lifeline: He authored the disastrous nuclear deal that gave the mullahs millions in cash and a clear path to build nuclear weapons.

Just days before that deal was signed, Iran's president marched with a huge crowd of Iranians who were holding "Death to Israel" and "Death to America" signs. That alone should have trumpeted the fact that the Western world—especially America—was humiliated through that deal.

Mr. Obama's support for the Iranian regime cannot be explained logically. Such a catastrophic policy can only be understood in the context of the *satanic deception* that blankets this *entire world* (Revelation 12:9).

Donald Trump pulled America out of that disastrous deal. For four years he worked to restrain Iran and support Israel's defense. But when Joe Biden took office, he quickly resumed negotiating a new agreement with Iran on nuclear technology. He showed the same willingness to grant humiliating concessions, to give the terrorist state unfettered access to more than $100 billion in assets, and to leave Iran a clear path to legally pursue nuclear weapons.

This is madness! IRAN'S SUPREME LEADER BELIEVES THAT CAUSING A NUCLEAR CATACLYSM WILL HASTEN THE COMING OF HIS VERSION OF THE MESSIAH. NO OTHER NUCLEAR POWER THINKS LIKE THAT. IT MAKES NUCLEAR WAR INEVITABLE!

Nothing could please the devil more! "[T]hat old serpent, called the Devil, and Satan, which deceiveth the whole world" has his fingerprints all over these developments. He passionately hates mankind and loves causing the death of millions, even billions!

If you doubt that it is about human survival, just talk to the Jewish nation that Iran repeatedly says it wants to wipe off the map. Israel believes its *survival* rests on whether or not Iran gets a nuclear bomb!

ANTI-ISRAELISM

The Obama administration demonstrated in many ways that it dislikes the Jews. Israeli leaders recognized this. They *must* have asked why that administration harbored such antipathy for them. They don't understand—and even the people who have that bitter feeling toward them often don't understand why their own hatred is so deep.

In January 2013, President Obama nominated Chuck Hagel as secretary of defense. This man had consistently spoken out against Israel and *for* Palestinians, terrorists and Iran. He voted *against* sanctioning Iran to stop pursuing nuclear weapons. He refused to sign a letter asking the European Union to name Hezbollah a terrorist organization. He accused Israel of "sickening slaughter" and "the systematic destruction of an American friend: the country and people of Lebanon." He supported the "Saudi Peace Initiative" calling for Israel to forfeit the Golan Heights, the West Bank and parts of Jerusalem, including the Jewish Quarter.

Why would President Obama want to make this man secretary of defense? Here is journalist Melanie Phillips's profound answer: "What therefore is the factor that Obama brings to the West's dismal foreign-policy table as illustrated by these truly appalling choices? *Malice.* Against the West, and ALSO AGAINST THE ANCIENT CIVILIZATION THAT LIES AT THE HEART OF ITS MORAL CODES" (Dec. 22, 2012).

What is the ancient civilization that lies at the heart of America's moral codes? *She is talking about Judeo-Christian history—and the morality of* THE BIBLE. THIS BEGINS TO GET TO THE CORE REASON WHY THESE HORRIFIC DECISIONS ARE BEING MADE. THE OBAMA ANTIOCHUS GOAL IS TO "BLOT OUT" THE NAME OF ISRAEL"! Phillips was absolutely right in saying that OBAMA VIEWS THAT CIVILIZATION—ALONG WITH ITS MORAL LAW—WITH MALICE.

Caroline Glick wrote, "Obama wants to hurt Israel. He does not like Israel. He is appointing anti-Israel advisers and cabinet members not *despite* their anti-Israel positions, but *because* of them. ... OBAMA WANTS TO FUNDAMENTALLY TRANSFORM THE U.S. RELATIONSHIP WITH ISRAEL. ... [T]he most urgent order of business for Israelis is to STOP DELUDING OURSELVES IN THINKING

THAT UNDER OBAMA THE U.S. CAN BE TRUSTED" (FrontPage Magazine, Dec. 17, 2012).

Jesus Christ spoke of "the times of the Gentiles" (Luke 21:24)—the culmination of the fall of the Israelite nations and the rise of Gentile powers in the Great Tribulation. In a way, Barack Obama brought the times of the Gentiles into America and enabled the Gentiles to cause terrible problems for the whole world!

Never did America direct such a hateful foreign policy toward our best ally in the Middle East. How can you explain that? A deeper historical look at Antiochus tells.

ANTIOCHUS'S WAR ON ISRAEL

In 168 B.C., Antiochus pillaged and desecrated the Jews' temple in Jerusalem. Josephus recorded that Antiochus "came up to Jerusalem, and, pretending peace, he got possession of the city by treachery; at which time he spared not so much as those that admitted him into it, on account of the riches that lay in the temple; but, led by his covetous inclination, (for he saw there was in it a great deal of gold, and many ornaments that had been dedicated to it of very great value,) and in order to plunder its wealth, he ventured to break the league he had made. So he left the temple bare, and took away the golden candlesticks, and the golden altar [of incense], and table [of shewbread], and the altar [of burnt offering]; and did not abstain from even the veils, which were made of fine linen and scarlet. He also emptied it of its secret treasures, and left nothing at all remaining; and by this means cast the Jews into great lamentation, for he forbade them to offer those daily sacrifices which they used to offer to God, according to the law."

Antiochus wanted to blot out that religion! *Imagine* how this would eviscerate the Jews emotionally and spiritually! After emptying the temple, Antiochus rededicated it as a shrine to Zeus, built a new altar over the one he had destroyed, and in the place of the daily sacrifice he ordered pigs to be sacrificed.

This was an egregious affront to God and the Jews. This made Antiochus worse than any prior king or emperor who had attacked Jerusalem. He desecrated the temple, insulting God and His people whose lives were to be tied to worshiping God according to His law. But even that was only the beginning!

Antiochus ordered his soldiers to kill those they met and anyone who took refuge in their homes. Infants, the elderly, women and children—any and all whom the soldiers could find were slaughtered. The apocryphal book of 2 Maccabees records that in three days, 40,000 people were slain and another 40,000 were taken into slavery!

After he left Jerusalem, Antiochus began to think of a "final solution" for dealing with the Jews. That term was used by the Nazis to describe the Holocaust of the Jews in World War II. Their final solution was to kill all the Jews they could, and by the end of that war, 6 million Jews were murdered. Some 60 million people died in that war altogether because of a Satan-possessed Antiochus—Adolf Hitler!

Anciently, Antiochus's final solution was just as evil, if not worse. He knew he couldn't exterminate the Jewish people completely, though he definitely killed many. Instead, his final solution was to exterminate the *faith* of Israel. He tried to blot it out from the face of the Earth!

"Throughout the turbulent changes of its past history," Werner Keller wrote in *The Bible as History,* "Israel had been spared none of the horror and ignominy which could befall a nation. But never before, neither under the Assyrians nor under the Babylonians, had it received such a blow as the edict issued by Antiochus Epiphanes by which he hoped to *crush and destroy the faith of Israel.*"

Antiochus ordered the compulsory paganizing of all Jews. The *Anchor Bible* says he tried to enforce his Hellenization policy upon the Jews even to the extent of completely *exterminating* them and their religion. No ancient king had ever tried to do such a thing.

Antiochus's hatred was above and beyond anything normal.

Antiochus was a tool in Satan's hands, just as the modern Antiochus is in this end time. The devil hates Jews, because God made them His scepter people (Genesis 49:10). Satan hates Israel and God's plan. Antiochus hated the Jews because Satan was so close to him, and he to Satan.

Today, that hatred is intensified. There really is a being who rules this world, and if he can get enough power over the people, they develop rabid hatred for *anything* related to the true God!

Daniel 11:22 in the Moffatt translation reads, "The opposing forces shall be swept before him and shattered, and so shall God's high priest." Antiochus went so far as to murder the Jewish high priest, Onias III, in 172 B.C.

Rulers before Antiochus had typically treated the Jews well. Antiochus was ruthless toward them in a way his predecessors had never been (verse 24). And that is only a type of the affliction coming upon three nations of Israel in this end time!

Verse 30 says Antiochus was deceitful with certain people *inside* the temple. We saw that happen in God's Church. This man found some people "inside the temple" who would betray God, and he allied himself with them and had "indignation against the holy covenant."

The "abomination that maketh desolate" in verse 31 is an *army* that smashes Jerusalem. It desecrates the holy place and takes away the daily sacrifice (see also Daniel 8:11, 24). This happened in 167 B.C. Tradition says Antiochus built a statue of Jupiter Olympus in the holy of holies—the holiest place inside the temple.

According to George Rawlinson, the Jews "were driven to desperation by the mad project of this self-willed monarch," speaking of Antiochus. In a sense, this is happening to a degree with the Jewish State of Israel today.

BLOTTING OUT ISRAEL

Again, 2 Kings 14:26-27 reveal the *real aim* of what Barack Obama has been doing and continues to do through the Biden administration: to "BLOT OUT THE NAME OF ISRAEL FROM UNDER HEAVEN." This gets to the truth in a way that no one else can recognize. "Under heaven" means the entire Earth! That is the extent of their blotting out the name of Israel. Everything is happening in a way that causes maximum destruction to the modern-day nations of Israel. And the only thing to prevent this is *God's intervention.*

The real mastermind is Satan the devil. He is the one who "made the earth to tremble"! (Isaiah 14:16). A human being could NOT plan out these events to create such scale of devastation. The devil, however, is extraordinarily shrewd and skilled at sabotage and destruction.

Ephesians 2:2 calls Satan "the prince of the power of the air, THE SPIRIT THAT NOW WORKETH IN THE CHILDREN OF DISOBEDIENCE." Yes, this evil spirit WORKS in people! He is able to influence people's thinking and emotions. The more that human beings allow themselves to be influenced by him, the more power they have to do terrible things!

Can you recognize the Afghanistan disaster as the earth-shaking event that it was? Can you see just how disastrous so many of the actions this administration is taking are—how monumentally destructive to America and the world?

This should shake us all to our core and cause us to acknowledge that GOD IS CURSING AMERICA!

Ultimately, this is not caused by a bad president. It is not even caused by the wickedness of the radical left. It is caused by GOD CURSING US FOR THE SINS OF THE WHOLE NATION. We ALL need to turn to God in repentance! We as a people are disobeying God and are facing the terrifying consequences. And because we refuse to acknowledge this, these wretched events are going to get far worse before this is over.

God has given America incomparable blessings, and He wants to continue to bless us. But He cannot do so while we live in rebellion against Him. He is correcting us—as a father who loves his children (e.g. Hebrews 12:5-7).

And 2 Kings 14:27 indicates that, even if we fail to repent collectively, in His mercy, God will ensure that the name of Israel is not BLOTTED OUT! He is going to save America, just as He saved our ancestors, "by the hand of Jeroboam"—temporarily.

The Bible provides the keys to understand these otherwise incomprehensible events. As Amos 3:7 says, "Surely the Lord GOD will do nothing, but he revealeth his secret unto his servants the prophets." God explains all these truths so we can recognize what is happening, heed His warnings, and turn from our sins! He also gives the outline of where these events will lead so we can SEE GOD'S HAND in what is happening as events unfold according to His prophecies.

Every American needs to recognize this and act on it! Regardless of what happens nationally, God gives you the power and the choice to do so individually.

CHAPTER TEN

DONALD TRUMP WILL FIGHT HIS WAY BACK

T HE DEVIL HAS SUCCESSFULLY USED THE RADICAL LEFT TO attack America. 2 Kings 14:26-27 show there are people working to blot out the name of Israel—and many of them are *inside America.* This alone helps us understand the seriousness of America's affliction today.

But God says in verse 27 that He "saved them by the hand of Jeroboam." Today, Donald Trump is fulfilling the role of an end-time "Jeroboam." God sent President Trump specifically to deal with that evil and actually *save* America temporarily. *This happened* during Donald Trump's first presidential term.

But that is not the end of the story. Mr. Trump has been pushed out of office, and now the *affliction* is worse than ever!

You have to realize that God is *invested* in this Trump presidency. God Himself sent Mr. Trump to keep the name of Israel from being blotted out because of satanically led people. And the work He has for this end-time Jeroboam is not complete.

This prophecy, in conjunction with Amos 7, foretells that Donald Trump is going to regain the presidency.

THE REASON FOR GOD'S ANGER

Let's study the pivotal prophecy in Amos 7.

It is extremely important that you understand the *context* of verses 1-6. These verses are tied directly to verses 7-17. All these verses lead us into the Great Tribulation and the Day of the Lord, which are concluded by the Second Coming of Jesus Christ! So this is all happening in the end of the *last hour* of the end time. Christ said when He was on Earth that we should know when these events are "at the door" (Matthew 24:33).

In Amos 7, God is *ferociously angry* and ready to send the end-time nations of Israel into World War III. He is about to allow them to experience the consequences of their mountainous, terrible sins and to be destroyed, enslaved and slaughtered!

I BELIEVE VERSES 1-6 OF AMOS 7 REVEAL SOMETHING SPECTACULAR ABOUT GOD'S THINKING AT THIS VERY MOMENT. THEY SURELY SHOW HOW EAGER OUR GOD OF LOVE IS TO GET THIS END-TIME HORROR OVER WITH!

We are in the outer edge of the storm that will usher in the Second Coming of Christ. GOD IS INTENSELY EXCITED FOR THAT TIME OF HAPPINESS AND UNPARALLELED JOY THAT IS ABOUT TO SATURATE THIS EARTH! I hope you think about this as you read the first six verses and then the rest of Amos 7.

In verses 1-3, God showed Amos a vision of *violent destruction*—a horde of locusts about to ravage the land. But Amos spoke up, and God changed His mind. That is astounding!

Then it happened a second time: "Thus hath the Lord GOD shewed unto me: and, behold, the Lord GOD called to *contend by fire,* and it devoured the great deep, and did eat up a part" (verse 4). This is a prophetic vision of a devouring *nuclear fire!* "Then said I, O Lord GOD, cease, I beseech thee: by whom shall Jacob arise? for *he is small.* The LORD repented for this: This also shall not be, saith the Lord GOD" (verses 5-6). Again God relented.

Notice this important thing, without which we cannot understand this passage: God did not say *why* He was so fiercely wrathful. The *context* provides the answer.

Starting in verse 7 is a crucial end-time prophecy about Jeroboam. It describes a time when Jeroboam—Donald Trump—

is in power. But the first 6 verses of the chapter are talking about the time when the man in power is *Antiochus.*

What makes God angry here is the work of an Antiochus!

The evil of this man is deplorable and infuriating. What he is doing to this country makes me sick and very angry. And if that is the way so many of us feel, how do you suppose *God* feels about it? God says that "the whole head is sick, and the whole heart faint" in America and the other end-time nations that descended from ancient Israel (Isaiah 1:5). These nations have received immense blessings and honor. Yet in the *superpower* of Israel, America, *Satan himself is ruling* through his man! Everything he does is aimed at destruction! He is "fundamentally transforming the United States of America" in the most diabolical ways!

Now he and his fellow leftists are not even disguising themselves as angels of light—they are being much more open and blatant because they have so much power. Yet *still* most people are asleep!

The country we live in is not what it used to be. When America was at its peak, and even as recently as Presidents Ronald Reagan or George W. Bush, it would not have been true to say that "Jacob"—mainly the United States—"is small." The nation still held prestige and power, and it is *still* the superpower of Israel. Yet when Barack Obama is in control, we are powerless! He and those he leads are doing Satan's work! There is nothing so terrifying. This man has the weight of the big corporations, Hollywood, academia and the media behind him, and he and his people will do anything they can get away with. Jacob really is "small"—powerless!

How could God NOT be upset by this?

Remember, it was "by reason of transgression"—the sins of the people—that this Antiochus was even able to attain rule (Daniel 8:12). And even with his destructive actions so overt, those with the power to stop him are too faint-hearted and weak, and millions of Americans enthusiastically *support* him!

Our people were given birthright blessings because of the great Abraham, the father of the faithful, who obeyed and was willing to sacrifice even his own son for God! Sadly, THEY HAVE TURNED THEIR BACKS ON GOD AND ARE FOLLOWING THE DEVIL.

The disaster spoken of in Amos 7:1-2 is the first presidential term of Barack Obama. Verse 4 describes his second presidential term. And *now* you can add to that his third term in which he is the puppet master of the Biden regime. This terribly upsets God! Obama has too much power, and God is going to have to do something. He has already started to act. God will not let him blot out the name of Israel!

GOD'S FINAL WARNING

There are three visions here, starting in verses 1, 4 and 7 of Amos 7, which all describe God "showing" Amos something. The two visions in verses 1-6 flow right into the vision of verses 7-17.

But just before verse 7, you could insert 2 Kings 14:26-28: "For the LORD saw the affliction of Israel, that it was very bitter: for there was not any shut up, nor any left, nor any helper for Israel. And the LORD said not that he would blot out the name of Israel from under heaven: but he saved them by the hand of Jeroboam the son of Joash. Now the rest of the acts of Jeroboam, and all that he did, and his might, how he warred, and how he recovered Damascus, and Hamath, which belonged to Judah, for Israel, are they not written in the book of the chronicles of the kings of Israel?" That gives you the whole context.

God already used President Trump once to save this nation from what Antiochus was doing. Now Obama, through Joe Biden, has returned with a vengeance. But *the rest of this prophecy in Amos 7 shows that will not last.*

When Amos saw those first two visions, he pleaded with God for mercy. Verses 2 and 3 in the Moffatt translation read, "As they devoured all the green growth, I cried, 'Have mercy, Lord, have mercy! How can Jacob recover?—he has so little.'" And God changed His mind: "Then the Eternal did relent, the Eternal said, 'This shall not be'" (Moffatt). The same thing appears in verse 6: "[T]he Eternal said, 'This shall not be.'"

But verse 8 is a different story: "The Eternal said to me, 'Amos, what do you see?' 'A plumb-line,' I replied. The Eternal said, 'With a plumb-line I test my people; *never again* will I pardon them'" (Moffatt). This is God talking! He essentially tells Amos, *Don't talk to me about this again!*—referring back to verses 3 and 6. This message today, prophesied in the book of Amos, is God's *last warning.* He has warned the Americans and other descendants of ancient Israel several times to try to wake them up, but they have ignored those warnings. So, He says, *I'll warn one last time!*

This is prophesying of the time just ahead of us. This will be the last time God passes by, so He is clearing the way for His Church to *finalize* this last warning. When America falls, a horrific chain reaction will unfold. God knew this and showed this terrifying future to Amos. He heard Amos's plea for mercy—twice. This flows right into verses 7-10; it is part of the same vision. God shows Amos a plummet and says He will measure one more time and give one last warning. After that He would *never* give them another warning, and He told Amos not to even ask Him again to change His mind.

We are in the *last time* God will pass by the people of Israel before they are destroyed! This is a time of extreme urgency!

Notice: This is in the context of an end-time *Jeroboam* (verse 9). It is during the time of Jeroboam that God says, "I will not again pass by them any more" (verse 8). God passes by for the *last time* to show three end-time nations of Israel—the United States, Britain and the Jewish nation—how to solve their problems and to warn them of the consequences of their failure to do so.

This prophecy means that PRESIDENT TRUMP WILL SOON RECOVER HIS PRESIDENCY. A stolen election, and a presidency, will be recovered. We will see Mr. Trump back in power soon. That will be positive, for a little while. Things will quickly improve in some ways—but only briefly; the curses will remain.

When that happens, Americans will be down to their *last time* to repent.

God's message through Amos and other prophetic books in the Bible, and now through the *Trumpet,* the *Key of David* and our other means, is about to go out for the *last time* before the destruction comes. If people don't repent, God will not pass by and warn any more! America will face the consequences of our sins! Yet in the end, as we will see, even that bad news will make people come to know God.

WHAT AMOS 7 DOES NOT SAY

Amos 7 prophesies about end-time Israel, which is today, most prominently, the United States superpower. It is clearly about the *very end* of the nation. It shows that at that time, Jeroboam is not only in power, but he is wielding kingly authority.

These verses describe the Prophet Amos's message from God to King Jeroboam. They also describe God's message today, which we will soon send to the modern Jeroboam!

If you read through this prophecy, THERE APPEARS TO BE NO BREAK IN JEROBOAM'S REIGN. It doesn't describe his presidency being lost and then somehow being restored. Why is that?

BECAUSE IN GOD'S VIEW, DONALD TRUMP NEVER LOST THE PRESIDENCY! By keeping the flow about Jeroboam going in this prophecy, IT SEEMS GOD IS SHOWING US THAT THE ELECTION WAS STOLEN! HE LOOKS ON MR. TRUMP AS STILL BEING THE RIGHTFUL PRESIDENT OF THE UNITED STATES!

Democrats spent all four years of President Trump's tenure trying to bring him down, and in the election, they finally succeeded. Politicians and the media did their best to cover it up. *But God saw it all.* He is the only one who knows precisely what happened.

Many millions of Americans believe, as I do, that the election was stolen. That view has far more weight if that's the way God Himself sees it!

The radical left has a track record of cheating, stealing and lying. Anyone who acts that way shows that their father is the devil! (John 8:44). America's Constitution was never intended to work for such people. It was made for a moral and religious people—not people who lie, cheat, steal and commit violence as a way of life. They don't believe in God, the Constitution or America.

One thing is certain: God is going to bring Mr. Trump back. It's just a matter of *when.* If He didn't, the name of Israel would essentially be blotted out!

With radicals in power, how could anyone complete God's work of delivering the warnings of Amos to America and its leaders? When the devil is motivating people, God's work is their chief target! Already God *had* to intervene and stop the evil that was happening, or the name of Israel would have been blotted out—and GOD'S VERY ELECT AND THEIR WARNING MESSAGE ARE AT THE HEART OF THAT NAME OF SPIRITUAL ISRAEL!

Look at how leftists are now using their power in the media, technology companies and social media to silence anyone who disagrees with them. They are clamping down on free speech and trampling the supreme law of the land!

Our forefathers had to die to secure our freedom of speech and freedom of religion!

What kind of people are we dealing with? Those who are now in charge *stole the election.* Those criminals are fighting against the living God! You can be sure God will not let that stand. God's warning message is going to get out there. God *will not* let them blot out this work nor our message because we have a job to do. God opens doors that nobody can shut, and He will shut them when they need to be shut. So we will put it in God's hands and simply trust Him.

God knows the election was stolen, so He must have a plan to take care of it. God is about to do some massive exposing of that treasonous theft and of the other brazen crimes being committed today.

THE AFFLICTION INTENSIFIES

In Amos 7:8, God says He is giving the nation its final warning. Then verse 9 describes a time of desolation, wasting and the sword. God forewarns that He Himself "will rise against the house of Jeroboam with the sword." That is a major intensifying of the picture in verse 8.

I believe there is, in fact, a *pause* in the events between verses 8 and 9, and that we are in this prophesied pause now—after the election coup that stole the presidency from Mr. Trump but before he returns to power.

Look around today: This country is in a catastrophe! Radicals are destroying the nation, foolishly thinking that somehow they will be able to control these ruinous, anarchic forces they are unleashing. And this trouble is certain to lead to worse trouble.

"[T]he sanctuaries of Israel shall be laid waste," verse 9 says. The word *sanctuaries* is interesting; it refers to false churches that God will allow to be destroyed. But it could also mean something more. *Gesenius' Hebrew-Chaldee Lexicon* defines the word as "asylum," which is a place of protection, especially for those pursued by the law; or an institution for the destitute. *The Theological Wordbook of the Old Testament* states, "Metaphorically, the word is used to refer to a place of refuge ...." In the modern nations of Israel, it could be describing *sanctuary cities.* It could portray our sanctuary nation, where our leaders allow anyone and everyone to flow across the border. Many are looking for a better life, but others are violent members of gangs or cartels and smugglers bringing drugs, slaves and thousands of destitute people here. How can this "sanctuary nation" policy not tear this nation apart? Our leaders do not even screen them. Yet they insist that the nation spend *billions and billions of dollars* to manage this problem they are causing, even when we have $31 trillion in debt that we can never repay—debt that will *explode in our faces* at any time! This is fiscal, political and intellectual *insanity.* SOME AUTHORITIES BELIEVE AMERICA'S DEBT IS OUR GREATEST

NATIONAL SECURITY PROBLEM. But most people act like it is no problem at all. That is extremely dangerous ignorance.

Recognize what is really happening in this land. God says He will rise against the house of Jeroboam with a sword. This means the terrible state we are in now is about to get worse! After the radicals have catastrophically weakened this country, the result will not be what they expect. They won't even have the opportunity to build the new system they imagine: A sword—foreign attack—is coming! They have weakened the country for other nations to destroy it!

We must remember, too, that the rest of the country has many sins as well. It is not just those on the left.

God will bring President Trump back for one reason: to keep Satan and his political Antiochus from blotting out the very name of Israel.

2022 MIDTERMS

Polls before America's November 8, 2022, midterm elections indicated a "red wave" would sweep the country. With inflation soaring and Joe Biden's approval ratings tanking, everybody expected signal Republican victories that would bring majorities in the House and Senate, as well as governorships in more states.

They were wrong. Outside of Florida, the red wave didn't happen. About half an hour after polls closed, Nevada's two largest counties stopped counting ballots because election workers were overwhelmed by an avalanche of mail-in ballots. Arizona's largest county reported that 20 percent of its tabulating machines were malfunctioning. Georgia was hit with a mysterious last-minute ballot drop for Democrat Sen. Raphael Warnock. There was a blackout in the security camera footage in the Nevada election facility from 11 p.m. on Election Night to 7 a.m. the next morning. By the time it was resolved, the Democratic House candidate had moved ahead in the polls. They say the blackout was an accident, no cheating involved.

But somehow these "accidents" ALWAYS FAVOR THE DEMOCRATS! Several key races experienced anomalies with voting machines, delayed counts, suspicious ballot dumps and other concerning developments that virtually *all* broke for Democrats—and that all undermine confidence in the integrity of the elections. It was a sickening repeat of the problems that plagued the 2020 elections. These people are committing treason against this land! And they are getting away with it.

Democrats gloated. And Republicans, astoundingly, rather than challenging the irregularities, fighting for transparency, and investigating possible crimes, meekly accepted the results. *Almost all of them* completely ignored the glaring evidence of fraud! Post-election, all the talk among Republicans centered around questions like: *What did we do wrong? Did we back the wrong candidates? Was our messaging off? How could our predictions have been so flawed?*

And most of all, they said: *This is all Donald Trump's fault.*

That was certainly the narrative immediately pushed by Democrats and radicals: The biggest loser of this election was Trump. And Republicans agreed!

That was the biggest lesson they took from these elections: We have to dump Trump.

What happened in these elections brings the prophecy of 2 Kings 14:26-28 into even starker focus. We must pay attention to what God foretells here!

ELECTION FRAUD

It is stunning how successful the devil has been in BLOTTING OUT talk of election fraud in America. The Democrats insist there is "no evidence" of any wrongdoing. The media label anyone who brings it up as an "election denier" and an extremist. They have *intimidated* most of the nation into shutting up and pretending there are no problems. And tragically, shamefully, the great majority of "conservative" politicians and pressmen have gone along!

Satan has hung a *curtain of fear.* Those who are afraid to confront Obama, in reality, fear Satan the devil. Many others actually *enjoy* being on his team.

When he was campaigning for president in 2008, Barack Obama answered a question about how to prevent election fraud: "Well, I tell you what: It helps in Ohio that we have Democrats in charge of the machines." He was implying that *Republicans* would use those machines to rig the vote! Then he said, "Look, I come from Chicago. So I want to be honest: It's not as if it's just Republicans who have monkeyed around with elections in the past. Sometimes Democrats have, too. Whenever people are in power, they have this tendency to try to, you know, tilt things in their direction."

Yes—Obama is *very familiar* with election fraud and how voting machines can be manipulated. He continued, "That is why we have got to have, I believe, a voting rights division in the Justice Department that is nonpartisan and that is serious about investigating cases of vote fraud .... That's why we need paper trails on these new electronic machines, so that you actually have something that you can hang onto after you punched that letter to make sure it has not been hacked into. Those are all part of the process of making sure that our democracy works for everyone."

Today, this man has a very different message. Now that Democrats are in power, he insistently peddles the lie that electronic voting machines are perfectly trustworthy. And anyone who insists on paper trails and proof of election security is sidelined and silenced!

Obama says that "MAGA Republicans ... claim, without any evidence, that the 2020 election was stolen." Frankly, there has been a DELUGE of evidence! But people will not look into it. Even Fox News will not allow anyone to report on the subject.

The repressive silence on this momentous issue is of Satan the devil! It is not of God, who always champions TRUTH. It's not even of common sense! Can you *believe* the media won't even *talk about* a matter SO CRITICAL FOR NATIONAL SURVIVAL?

Donald Trump has said all along that the 2020 election was stolen, and he is absolutely right.

Mike Lindell is another of the few people who have been going after Barack Obama and those machines from the beginning. Far too few are listening to him and the evidence he has presented, but from the beginning, he said that if you don't get rid of the machines Democrats used to steal the 2020 election, you won't win another election. He is right! Look what is happening: The midterms should have been an absolute blowout victory for Republicans. But they weren't, and THIS IS WHY!

REPUBLICAN DIVISION

After the 2022 midterms, "conservative" news outlets like the *New York Post, Wall Street Journal* and Fox News began insisting that Republicans must "dump Trump" if they want to win elections. All three of these media outlets are owned by media mogul Rupert Murdoch, who believes Republicans need a new leader. Establishment Republicans blamed *Trump* for failures in the midterms. That is sheer nonsense! There is *no truth* in that.

Senate Minority Leader Mitch McConnell's high-spending super-PAC devoted vast amounts of money supporting anti-Trump Republicans like liberal Alaska senator Lisa Murkowski but spent next to nothing supporting pro-Trump Republicans like Arizona Senate candidate Blake Masters. He did this even though the Republican Party didn't need much help in Alaska but desperately needed help in Arizona. So it's pretty clear that McConnell and his supporters were more concerned about defeating the MAGA movement than defeating Democrats.

IT IS ASTOUNDING THAT THESE ESTABLISHMENT REPUBLICANS WOULD RATHER LIVE UNDER THE TYRANT BARACK OBAMA THAN SUPPORT SENATORS WHO BACK AND SUPPORT DONALD TRUMP! How can you deal with that kind of division? Such senseless decisions are political suicide! What is wrong with their minds? They have become addicted to the devil's reasoning.

These Republicans have divided their own party. If your army is fighting against itself, how many times are you going to win?

Mr. Trump helped Ron DeSantis become governor in Florida. DeSantis really should have expressed some gratitude, but he didn't say anything. He is a strong governor. Republicans are happy to have him on their side. But God isn't going to save America through anybody except Donald Trump.

People believed a red tsunami would shift power to Republicans. But they must face the fact that until they get rid of the machines, they will never win many elections. They are so naive. As LONG AS THOSE MACHINES ARE IN PLACE, THE RADICAL LEFT WILL STEAL ELECTIONS!

Former House Speaker Newt Gingrich pointed to a report showing that Republican votes for House candidates outnumbered Democrats by 5 million to 6 million votes, yet had little to show for it in terms of victories. "I've never been as wrong as I was this year," he said. "It makes me challenge every model I'm aware of." Appearing on Fox News, he said something just didn't seem right, but he stopped short of discussing the possibility of fraud—I'm sure because Fox News owner Rupert Murdoch shut that down! "Not gaining very many seats makes you really wonder what's going on," he said. "I want to know, where did those votes come from?"

I do believe that things going this way is a *blessing* for Republicans. God allowed the machines to run the course. He could have changed that. He could have had Republicans win everything. Perhaps, rather than giving them big victories, God is waking them up to the fact that the machines are corrupted. A trial like this may be the only way some of these people can be jolted to see reality: THIS IS A WAR.

There is a war for control of America. At the heart of it are the voting machines. Either get rid of the machines or forget about winning!

As the Prophet Isaiah wrote, "THE WHOLE HEAD IS SICK, AND THE WHOLE HEART FAINT." America's power structures are terminally ill, top to bottom. The government agents are sick; the legislators are sick; the judges are sick; the media moguls are sick; the officials counting our votes are sick. Why did it take officials in Clark County, Nevada, nearly a week to count 50,000 mail-in ballots when it should take less than a day?

The FBI seized Mike Lindell's phone after he tried to bring attention to voting machine irregularities. Former Trump adviser Peter Navarro was literally shackled after he highlighted mail-in ballot fraud. Do you think the Biden administration is going to let people look into what happened in Arizona, Nevada and elsewhere?

Satan certainly has a lot of help! But 2 Kings 14 shows that there is *no helper* for Israel. Mr. Lindell is so committed to exposing election fraud, he nearly lost his corporation. You don't find many people willing to make sacrifices like that. But he doesn't have any real power. There is no helper—no real power coming to the aid of President Trump and of America.

There's no helper there, except God! God sees everything that is happening. And these criminals are going to run up against something they have never faced before.

God is going to save Israel—otherwise Barack Obama would blot out the name of Israel!

Another detail in 2 Kings 14 gives us insight into what is happening during the pause in Trump's rule, between his first term and his restoration to power.

'WARRED' TO 'RECOVER'

2 Kings 14:26-27 describe the bitter affliction in America and how God "saved them by the hand of Jeroboam." As I said, this was fulfilled, at least in part, during President Trump's first term.

The next verse begins a new paragraph, as you can see in the King James Version: "Now the rest of the acts of Jeroboam, and all that he did, and his might, how he WARRED, and how he RECOVERED Damascus, and Hamath, which belonged to Judah, for Israel, are they not written in the book of the chronicles of the kings of Israel?" (verse 28). This verse marks a new development. It happens *after* God uses Jeroboam to save Israel.

This verse shows that the end-time Jeroboam has to wage war to recover his presidency. After using the word *saved* in verse 27, it uses another, even stronger word: *warred.* Jeroboam has to WAR to *recover* something.

In ancient Israel, King Jeroboam II reigned 41 years, but many Bible chronologists believe the first 12 years of his reign were a coregency with his father, Joash, when he WARRED against Syria. Often, what happened anciently is not exactly the same as what is prophesied to happen in the end time. Yet there is also some kind of *warring* or fighting in this end time. The fact that the verse about *warring* comes after the verse about *saving* indicates that the end-time Jeroboam wages "war" after he has already saved Israel once. There are several different ways in which God could use Jeroboam to *war* today.

Gesenius' Lexicon says the word "warred" means "to fight, to war." *The Theological Wordbook of the Old Testament* says that *warring* "occurs 171 times, pertain[ing] to God's role in Israel's wars." That would apply in this case, because God has commissioned Mr. Trump to save Israel. Consider how different this word is from "saved" in verse 27. Mr. Trump did not have to WAR to save Israel during his first term—though he did have to fight to expose all the fraudulent investigations, impeachments and other treasonous actions. There are different ways "war" could apply, but the indication is that regaining office may take considerable fighting. Donald Trump will have to fight for it. It doesn't have to involve military action, but it certainly *could.*

Verse 28 of 2 Kings 14 strongly indicates that Mr. Trump *recovers* his presidency by some kind of *warring*—this strongly indicates more than just voting! It seems certain to me that this will happen *before* the next presidential election in 2024—unless there would be some kind of warring and voting combined. But 2 Kings 14:28 does not even *hint* of an election.

There is going to be some kind of war to recover something. In order to return to power, Mr. Trump is going to have to war! There are very few people warring with him today. But I don't care how much his enemies hate him—PROPHECY SAYS TRUMP WILL RETURN. We have said that from the very beginning of the 2020 election. If God says President Trump is going to "recover" something, then it will be recovered. Amos 7 also shows that war will be successful. And what could he *recover*, if not the stolen election?

This all must happen because of a miracle from God! And that should be obvious to everybody when it happens, if they are honest.

On November 15, 2022, Trump announced his candidacy for the 2024 presidential election. In his speech he said, "Together, we will be taking on the most corrupt forces and entrenched interests imaginable. ... Our country is being destroyed before your very eyes. ... The Washington establishment wants to silence us, but we will not let them do that. ... We will be attacked. We will be slandered. We will be persecuted .... But we will not be intimidated. We will persevere. We will stand tall in the storm. We will march forward into the torrent, and we, in the end, will win. Our country will win."

After all the terrible attacks on this man for the past six years, it is remarkable that he has the stamina and determination and fight to keep doing battle for this country. He is a man ready for war.

You need to watch Jeroboam. He is going to WAR HIS WAY BACK.

'THE KINGDOM'S COURT'

One detail in Amos's prophecy could provide a clue as to how Donald Trump will recover the presidency.

When in Amos 7:13 Amaziah says "it is the king's court," the word "king's" means *kingdom*. The King James Version margin reads, "house of the kingdom." Wycliffe translates it, "house of the realm." This is *the nation's* house. It is not something that is *following* Jeroboam, yet it *favors* him. It is helping him in some way. What is this referring to prophetically?

I believe this is referring to the United States Supreme Court.

This court was designed to guard the supreme law of the land, the Constitution. In many ways, the Supreme Court is over the whole nation. Even the president is subject to it—which is exactly the type of entity that the "house of the kingdom" is referring to.

I believe this prophetic account in Amos 7 implies that there is a conservative advantage in the Supreme Court, one that favors Jeroboam. During his presidency, Donald Trump selected three justices: Neil Gorsuch, Brett Kavanaugh and Amy Coney Barrett. It turned the orientation of the court more conservative. This could work to help fulfill this prophecy.

Justice Kavanaugh's confirmation process in 2018 was a calamitous display of lawlessness and disorder in America. Leftists tried to convince the public that Kavanaugh was a sexual predator. Democrats showed themselves willing to crawl in the gutter to prevent conservatives from gaining a Supreme Court majority. Angry citizens personally confronted public officials and screamed in their faces. It was probably the ugliest, most embarrassing spectacle in modern American politics. It demonstrated the stranglehold the devil has gained over the radical left. Yet despite the tumult, Kavanaugh was actually confirmed. Radicals want to control the courts, especially the Supreme Court, and God upset those plans. He has a plan of His own.

Similar vitriol was hurled at Justice Barrett during her confirmation process in October 2020. Democrats howled that it was illegitimate for President Trump to nominate her, and Republican senators to confirm her, so close to the end of Trump's presidential term. Yet she too took her place on the court.

After the 2020 presidential election, several cases came before the Supreme Court that could have helped overturn the fraud that had been committed, yet in every case the court declined to hear them. This demonstrated the justices' lack of courage and underscored the fact that there is not "any helper for Israel" (2 Kings 14:26).

However, we cannot overlook the statement in the prophecy of Amos 7 about the role of "the kingdom's court." The way this is written, this individual, Amaziah, is speaking on behalf of King Jeroboam, who has the support of "the king's chapel"—likely a reference to the support Donald Trump enjoys from many evangelicals and other religious people—and "the kingdom's court"—the Supreme Court. This reference strongly suggests to me that the court will play a decisive role in returning Mr. Trump to the presidency.

Somebody needs to take a case against the voting machines to the Supreme Court. Amos 7:13 indicates that it is that court that will make the decision. Then God can get Mr. Trump into office. That will surely happen soon.

In the speech announcing his 2024 candidacy, Trump called this period out of office a "pause." "One of the important factors of THE PAUSE is that we see how bad they've done, so we will be able to do it properly and it will be much easier," he said. "Everybody will agree with us because everybody sees what a bad job has been done during this two-year period." Again, I believe there is a PAUSE in events between Amos 7:8 and 9—after the election coup but before Mr. Trump returns to power.

Yes, evil forces are working to blot out the name of Israel. Satan will keep pushing this destructive agenda until God stops him—and ultimately confines him to the abyss!

HELPING JUDAH

2 Kings 14:28 states that Jeroboam recovered Damascus and Hamath. The *Soncino* commentary states that Damascus was once ruled by King David, and that the king of Hamath paid tribute to David and became part of his son Solomon's kingdom (2 Samuel 8:9-10; 1 Kings 8:65). So the indication is that Jeroboam reclaimed something to help Judah.

Here is how the New International Version translates 2 Kings 14:28: "As for the other events of Jeroboam's reign, all he did, and his military achievements, including how he recovered for Israel both Damascus and Hamath, which had belonged to Judah, are they not written in the book of the annals of the kings of Israel?" The Ferrar Fenton translation reads, "For the other affairs of Jerabam, and all that he did, how he warred, and how he recaptured Damascus and Khamath of Judah to Israel, they are recorded in the history of events of the days of the kings of Israel."

When Barack Obama was president, he was terribly unmerciful to the Jewish nation of Israel. But in President Trump's first term, he saved the Jewish nation of Israel (biblical Judah) from much of Obama's tyranny. He supported Israel in many ways, including scrapping the Iran deal, moving the U.S. Embassy to Jerusalem, and helping Israel sign the "Abraham Accords" with Arab nations in the region. Columnist Lee Smith described the alliance between Israel and the Gulf states as "an impediment to *the dream of a reempowered, nuclear-armed Iran backed by the United States,* WHICH WAS OBAMA'S MAIN FOREIGN-POLICY AIM—and an affront to peace processors convinced of their own never-ending importance. The Biden administration apparently aims to sink the accords by penalizing Israel and its peace partners for getting too close, and returning the Palestinians to center stage—in order to prepare the ground for reentering the Iran deal" (*Tablet,* March 21, 2021).

Note that: "Obama's main foreign-policy aim" was to align America with Iran—Israel's enemy, America's enemy and the world's number one terrorist-sponsoring nation! For America to support Iran makes no sense, *unless* you realize that AMERICA'S LEADER IS TRYING TO BLOT OUT THE NAME OF ISRAEL. And now, that policy is back! Biden is empowering Iran so it can soon obtain nuclear weapons.

From the time of Joe Biden's inauguration, I predicted that we would have more Palestinian terrorist attacks because of the change in leadership. That is exactly what began to happen. Anybody should be able to recognize why!

God is wrathful about this. If this continues, it will end very badly! You see how important it is that somebody "recover" something.

There is also a connection here to God's work. Isaiah 40:9 shows that God's Church in this end time has a message that must be delivered to "the cities of Judah": "BEHOLD YOUR GOD!" Much of that message revolves around our archaeological discoveries, led by the late Dr. Eilat Mazar. We have supported archaeology projects in Jerusalem for the past 50 years, and we even had the privilege to help uncover King David's palace! Now God's Church possesses the new throne of David (request a free copy of my book *The New Throne of David*). This work has a vitally important message that the Jews *need* to hear as a witness in this end time!

Satan knows this. He and his Antiochus are working fiercely to *blot out* our message, which is the ultimate expression of "the name of Israel."

It appears Mr. Trump may have to recover some of Judah's freedom for God's Church to even be able to deliver God's message to the cities of Judah.

A CHANGE IN ANTIOCHUS

The end of Jeroboam's life and reign are recorded in 2 Kings 14:29: "And Jeroboam slept with his fathers, even with the kings of Israel; and Zachariah his son reigned in his stead." This too indicates a restoration to the presidency for Donald Trump. He will recover power, but not for long. That is when the rest of Amos 7 will be fulfilled.

Notice something else implied in this chapter.

God commissions His prophet to issue a very tough warning message: "And the high places of Isaac shall be desolate, and the sanctuaries of Israel shall be laid waste; and I will rise against the house of Jeroboam with the sword" (Amos 7:9). This message will provoke a confrontation: "Then Amaziah the priest of Bethel sent to Jeroboam king of Israel, saying ..." (verse 10).

This verse introduces a religious leader named Amaziah. Who is this? It is actually *another* Antiochus—the one who infiltrated God's own Church!*

WHAT HAPPENED TO THE POLITICAL ANTIOCHUS? There is a definite shift here that suggests a major change in America. We are entering into a different era. The earlier verses prophesied of the Antiochus in the nation, who is fighting to destroy Jeroboam, then suddenly we have *another* Antiochus who is fighting to try to help Jeroboam *survive.* Thus we see that Satan forsakes one of his Antiochus types and jumps to another!

From Amos 7:7 on, we see no hint of the political Antiochus (Barack Obama). Will God remove him when Jeroboam "wars"? Will that be the end of the political Antiochus's real power? God does not say definitely, but I believe Amos 7 strongly indicates it. There are certain to be some big changes.

God's Church battled a spiritual Antiochus who took power and used it to almost blot out the Church. Now we have been battling the political Antiochus as he attacks America. Then suddenly we have to battle the spiritual Antiochus in God's Church again, and this time he has some kind of connection to the reempowered Jeroboam.

What does this *spiritual* Antiochus say? "Amos hath conspired against thee in the midst of the house of Israel: the land is not able to bear all his words" (verse 10). What a statement! The message from God's faithful people, part of which you are reading right now, will reach a point that the people cannot BEAR it and want it STOPPED!

Amid all these terrible events, there is a Church with a powerful message exposing everything, and in such a way that the people cannot bear it!

In verse 11, Amaziah says, "For thus Amos saith, Jeroboam shall die by the sword [that's not true; Amos said God would *rise against* the *house of Jeroboam* with a sword], and Israel

---

* This is explained in Appendix A: "Prophetic Duality."

shall surely be led away captive out of their own land." Other prophecies show that there will be a fierce trade war that will keep mounting until one third of our people are dead or starving; then will come a nuclear attack, which will kill another third. After two thirds of the people are dead, the final third will be led away captive. Those truths are hard for people to bear! But we have been prophesying this for over 75 years. Now we are very close to its fulfillment.

Prophecy shows that Satan, after attacking spiritual Israel (the Church) with an Antiochus, then physical Israel (America in particular) with a political Antiochus, will use a THIRD Antiochus, a dictator over a mighty foreign empire, to war against and *kill* millions, especially within spiritual Israel and physical Israel. This man is rising right now in Europe. With the Catholic Church, he will help resurrect the Holy Roman Empire. As it has done repeatedly throughout history, this empire will kill and kill, especially Americans and other descendants of Israel—and *especially* lukewarm people in God's Church who turned away from Him. They will kill God's people and believe they are doing God's work! (See John 16:2.)

Amaziah's message continues: "Also Amaziah said unto Amos, O thou seer, go, flee thee away into the land of Judah, and there eat bread, and prophesy there: But prophesy not again any more at Bethel: for it is the king's chapel, and it is the king's court" (Amos 7:12-13). Here is a KING with a *chapel* and a *court*. He is in charge, with kingly authority! Everything seems to be going well for him. God is going to give him the power to save Israel until this message of warning is finished.

But with that power, this man will actually authorize the banishment of God's people—an end-time Amos-type work—from the country and exile them to Israel, the Jewish nation in the Middle East!

This aligns with other prophecies that God's people will be sent to a place of safety, protected by God during the time of "great tribulation" (Matthew 24:21) that destroys America and

Britain. This will be a challenging time for God's people, but we know the end result is also prophesied, and we are excited. Who *wouldn't* want to live at the time when these wicked governments of men finally fall and Jesus Christ returns, as He promised, to take over the governance of all mankind? What a time to be alive!

Right now, the big question regarding fulfilled prophecy is *how* Donald Trump will regain power. America is in the throes of an Antiochus regime that is rapidly driving the nation toward radicalism, socialism, amorality, class division, civil war and outright destruction. In 2 Kings 14:26, America's affliction is very bitter, and the nation has no helper!

But God's prophecies are sure. And Jeroboam's clash with God's Church in Amos 7 is clear. This has not happened yet; therefore, President Trump must regain office one way or another. The biggest indicator in the Bible that this will occur is the end-time prophecy of Amos 7. We are now in the time frame of this prophetic chapter.

A TIME OF EXTREME URGENCY

Right now, there is a great focus on whether Donald Trump will return to office. Prophecy shows that he will. The bigger issue is what will happen *after* Trump regains power. He will stop the blotting out of the name of Israel. But this nation is very far from God! And Jeroboam and everyone else need a *powerful* warning and a call to repentance.

We do not know exactly how this will unfold. But keep watching Donald Trump, because he is not finished. It is not enough to just recognize the evil being perpetrated by the radical left. Nor should you put your faith in Donald Trump, the modern-day Jeroboam. You must have faith in, and repent toward, the God who used Trump and is about to use him again—or the curse on America will continue.

Watch as these dramatic prophecies unfold. See God's hand in these events. And let that motivate you to seek Him and allow

Him to rule your life! God says He will pass by one last time! People will either receive this message now and repent, or God will plunge them into the Great Tribulation.

Amos "warned the people that the supreme moment of their success was but the prelude to their doom" (*Soncino* commentary). This is what we are looking at when Donald Trump resumes the presidency. It will actually be a prelude to America's doom!

President Trump's return will "save America" briefly. But he will have to hear God's message and realize that GOD saved America *through* him—and that he and this nation must repent, believe and OBEY. If the American people do not repent and turn back to God during Trump's second term, then God will allow America to become "desolate" and "laid waste."

Even his own house God will destroy by the sword! Conditions in America may improve for a short time. But its ultimate end is destruction. Our people are going to face the wrath of God until they repent!

Amos 7:7-17 show that our time is very limited. What is going to happen in the coming months?

THIS IS ONE OF THE STRONGEST, MOST URGENT WARNINGS IN THE BIBLE!

That is what God's Church is here to provide, as loudly and clearly as we can. If the American people do not heed God's warning, they will suffer the consequences. But the good news is that this coming mass-scale violence is not just God's wrath—it is also His CORRECTION. That severe correction is what it will take for God to reach people, and humble them, in preparation for the return of Jesus Christ and the establishment of His Kingdom on Earth!

Prophecy by Jesus Christ and others in the Bible clearly states that even those who *die* having never known the one true God will later be *resurrected* to learn the consequences of sin, to repent and to finally know their God.

"Then answered Amos, and said to Amaziah, I was no prophet,

neither was I a prophet's son; but I was an herdman, and a gatherer of sycomore fruit" (verse 14). Amos had no formal seminary or college training. God simply gave him a job. Even without "credentials," this man was used by God.

Here is what he said to Amaziah: "Now therefore hear thou the word of the LORD: Thou sayest, Prophesy not against Israel, and drop not thy word against the house of Isaac. Therefore THUS SAITH THE LORD; Thy wife shall be an harlot in the city, and thy sons and thy daughters shall fall by the sword, and thy land shall be divided by line; and thou shalt die in a polluted land: and Israel shall surely go into captivity forth of his land" (verses 16-17). Amos had a very different view from Amaziah: He knew this was a message from God! And this Amaziah, who is also the religious Antiochus, is a man whom those in God's Church have faced before. We know who he is, just as we know that Barack Obama is the political Antiochus.

"Behold, the days come, saith the Lord GOD, that I will send a famine in the land, not a famine of bread, nor a thirst for water, but of hearing the words of the LORD" (Amos 8:11). How will this famine of the word come about? God's Church will be forced to leave. No one will be here to deliver the message anymore. When this faithful remnant of God's people leaves the country and is taken to a place of safety, God's message will cease, except what we do from there. The nations of Israel have had over 75 years to heed this message, but soon they will not be able to even find it.

Verse 14 talks about people who "shall fall, and never rise up again." This is talking about God's people—those who turned from God and refuse to repent—who will lose their eternal lives.

The great majority of Christians are not true Christians. That is why Christianity today is so self-contradicting, divided and weak. It is not biblical Christianity at all! That is part of God's warning to America and its (rightful) leader: More than 99 percent of Christians are deceived!

But some few *have* known God. Some of them will surely read this book. *Your physical and spiritual lives are on the line.*

REMEMBER THIS MESSAGE

"In that day will I raise up the tabernacle of David that is fallen, and close up the breaches thereof; and I will raise up his ruins, and I will build it as in the days of old" (Amos 9:11). This is a prophecy of God's end-time Church, built by Herbert W. Armstrong, destroyed by an Antiochus after his death, then raised up again through a faithful remnant. The story of how God "raise[d] up his ruins" is told in our free book *Raising the Ruins.*

It is this work that God puts in the middle of these climactic end-time events—"in the midst of my people Israel" (Amos 7:8). His people must be at the center telling the world what is happening and what it all means. This book is an important part of that.

We have a limited time to complete this work. God is showing us that we are drawing extremely close to the end. When God has passed by Israel for the last time, He will take His faithful remnant to a place of safety. If anyone is going to join them in that place of protection, this is their last chance—or they will face the fate of the house of Jeroboam!

Look at the context for Amos 7. "The words of Amos, who was among the herdmen of Tekoa, which he saw concerning Israel …. And he said, The Lord will roar from Zion, and utter his voice from Jerusalem …" (Amos 1:1-2). Who is going to be that voice? Which people will utter God's voice from spiritual Jerusalem? God has given us this message—we must proclaim it!

This nation and the world must be warned! Verse 2 concludes, "… and the habitations of the shepherds shall mourn, and the top of Carmel shall wither." The *Anchor Bible* says the subject here is a cosmic holocaust—a *nuclear* holocaust! God is about to send nuclear fire (see also verses 4, 7, 10, 12, 14; 2:2, 5).

The division in America is a sign of and a trigger for horrible times striking Americans and people from all nations. Our drastic rebellion against God is leading to drastic punishment. God is allowing us to see the results of worshiping our own will and, knowingly or unknowingly, following Satan. Our only hope is not in a political party or a man—even Jeroboam—but in God. And to truly have hope in God, you must not only believe in Him but also repent toward Him, submit to Him, and obey His law.

That is the lesson of history, the lesson of our nation's bitter affliction, and the lesson of these powerful, shocking, certain Bible prophecies.

As world conditions deteriorate and you see these dire prophecies fulfilled, *remember this message.* Even in a blistering message like Amos's, there is good news: This world racing to its destruction is a prophesied sign not only of the hopelessness of human nature itself but also of the arrival of a *new world!*

Yes, there are grim prophecies ahead, but THEY ALL LEAD TO THE RETURN OF JESUS CHRIST! The prophecy of Daniel 8 culminates in verse 25: "… he [the European Antiochus] shall also stand up against the Prince of princes [Christ Himself]; but he shall be broken without hand." Christ will smash all this evil and establish the rule of God on Earth! Revelation 12:9 and verse 12 say Satan has been cast down and he is full of wrath because he knows *his time is short.* That means the devil knows JESUS CHRIST IS ABOUT TO RETURN to dethrone him and bring men the peace, joy and happiness they ought to have. How encouraging!

If you acknowledge your sins and turn to God, He will lead you to repentance, forgive you, correct and guide you, protect you spiritually, and even protect you physically from the imminent, catastrophic Tribulation (verse 14). You will then help Jesus Christ reestablish God's government on Earth to *end* all this rebellion and deceit, and *end* all the suffering and death.

Contemplate the wonderful conclusion God gives us in Amos 9:13-15: "Behold, the days come, saith the Lord, that the plowman shall overtake the reaper, and the treader of grapes him that soweth seed; and the mountains shall drop sweet wine, and all the hills shall melt. And I will bring again the captivity of my people of Israel, and they shall build the waste cities, and inhabit them; and they shall plant vineyards, and drink the wine thereof; they shall also make gardens, and eat the fruit of them.

And I will plant them upon their land, and they shall no more be pulled up out of their land which I have given them, saith the Lord thy God."

This world does not know God—but they are about to get to know Him. They will finally have their chance to come out of deception, to repent and to grow spiritually until they achieve their incredible God-given potential. God will resurrect from the dead those who have already died and will die when these terrible prophecies come to pass; they will live again—under *God's* government.

Ultimately, even the bad news is good news. God is preparing the way for Israel and then the whole world to know Him! Soon, everyone will be educated in God's ways and blessed for their obedience.

Most people will never encounter God's message until the return of Jesus Christ or until that future resurrection beyond.

You have God's message in your hands right now.

Today is your day. Today is the time for you to repent and obey God. You have the unparalleled opportunity to give yourself to God, to give to His work, and to give to this world. Making that historic decision will affect your whole life, and so many more, now and for eternity.

Respond to God. Repent toward God. He will use *your life* to help lift America and the whole world out of crisis.

APPENDIX A

PROPHETIC DUALITY

A MAJOR KEY TO UNDERSTANDING THE BIBLE AND ITS PROPHE-cies is knowing that God works in dual stages. The first man, Adam, was a precursor to the second Adam, Jesus Christ (1 Corinthians 15:45-47). The Old Covenant predated and foreshadowed the New Covenant. The priesthood of ancient Israel typified New Testament Christians (1 Peter 2:5, 9). Christ's first coming foreshadowed His Second Coming. Biblical examples abound.

This vital key of duality unlocks many Bible prophecies. Often, there is a physical type and spiritual antitype. At other times, a preliminary fulfillment is only a forerunner of a latter, more dramatic fulfillment, usually occurring in the "time of the end," prior to the Second Coming of Jesus Christ. God says we must look at "former" events and "consider" them if we are to understand the "latter end" of His prophecies (Isaiah 41:22). THOUGH MANY PROPHECIES HAVE BEEN FULFILLED IN THE PAST, MOST OF THEM WERE ONLY A SMALL TYPE OF A GREATER END-TIME FULFILLMENT. MANY BIBLE SCHOLARS FAIL TO SEE THAT PAST, PARTIALLY FULFILLED PROPHECIES STILL HAVE AN END-TIME FULFILLMENT.

You can *prove* from your own Bible what I am saying. God teaches us to "prove all things" (1 Thessalonians 5:21).

This principle applies to certain prophecies related to America today.

Daniel 8 is an example we need to understand.

Verses 9-12 had an ancient fulfillment. Virtually all commentaries agree who the "little horn" in verse 9 is: Antiochus

Epiphanes, the ruthless Seleucid ruler who deceitfully obtained rule in Palestine in 176 B.C. and attempted to annihilate the Jews and their faith.

However, the last part of verse 17 shows that this prophecy is for "the time of the end," and verse 23 verifies that certain details will occur "in the latter time of their kingdom, when the transgressors are come to the full ...."

The Daniel 8 prophecy primarily focuses on *the Church of God.* This whole vision is about the daily sacrifices in the temple (verses 11-14). Today, in "the time of the end," the temple is God's Church (Ephesians 2:20-21).

This is another example of duality: The ancient nation of Israel was a forerunner of God's Church, which Scripture labels *spiritual* "Israel" (e.g. Galatians 6:16; Ephesians 2:12).

Perhaps you have no history with that Church. But what happened in spiritual Israel is still extremely relevant to you, and I will explain why.

IF YOU WANT TO KNOW HOW SATAN OPERATES, JUST LOOK AT WHAT HE DID TO GOD'S CHURCH.

The details of this prophecy have very personal, emotional meaning to me—because we dealt personally with the Antiochus inside the Church of God. Satan elevated that man to the highest office in the Church and used him to destroy it from within! Daniel 8:11 says this man "magnified himself even to [against] the prince of the host [Jesus Christ], and by him the daily sacrifice [the work of God] was taken away, and the place of his sanctuary was cast down." The devil used this Antiochus-type man *inside the Church of God* to destroy God's work. He acted like God and had the gall to magnify himself even against Jesus Christ! Only Satan could motivate a man to operate so boldly.

Verse 12 further describes this man's character: "And an host [a *demon army*] was given him against the daily sacrifice *by reason of transgression,* and it CAST DOWN THE TRUTH TO THE GROUND; and it practised, and prospered." From inside the Church, this man cast down the truth to the ground, changing the doctrines and kicking out anyone who disagreed. He was a lawless man! Moreover, his campaign of lawlessness was very successful. It was all "by reason of transgression," meaning revolt, rebellion, sin against lawful authority. The people in God's Church were sinning, so they lacked God's power. As a result, this army of demons was able to march in and destroy 95 percent of God's people spiritually.*

Verses 13 and 14 prophesied that the work of God's Church would be halted but then resume after 2,300 morning and evening sacrifices.** The work was raised up from the ruins by a faithful few who did not cast truth to the ground (Amos 9:11).

This whole story is told in our free book *Raising the Ruins.* I would like to give you a free copy. It is filled with details about what happened in God's Church after Herbert W. Armstrong died in 1986. That Church was devastated.***

This prophecy in Daniel 8 applies to God's Church. It also DIRECTLY APPLIES TO YOU. In this book, I am showing how this prophecy also applies to prophetic Israel, especially America. How can we know these nations are included in this prophecy?

The more you know about what happened in spiritual Israel, the Church, *the better you can understand the crisis in America.*

THAT ARMY OF DEMONS IS STILL AROUND. They wrecked the Church, and now they are wrecking NATIONS!

GREAT TRIBULATION

Look at verses 23 and 24 of Daniel 8. These verses specifically describe "a king of fierce countenance"—a strongman, a tyrant—rising up in the "latter time," "when the transgressors are come to the full." This aligns with several other biblical prophecies

---

* My free booklets *Daniel—Unsealed at Last!* and *Daniel Unlocks Revelation* explain this passage in detail.

** As I explain in *Daniel—Unsealed at Last!,* this equates to 1,150 days.

*** This history is also explained in detail, from a prophetic perspective, in my book *Malachi's Message to God's Church Today,* also free.

referring to a mighty political leader who is about to emerge to lead a terribly destructive European empire.

This man too is an end-time type of Antiochus. He will be somewhat in the mold of Adolf Hitler, yet far more subtle and smooth. He is a leader who understands "dark sentences" and is able to destroy mightily—"not by HIS OWN power," but by the devil's power. Many other prophecies show that God will use the European power this man leads—a final, latter-day resurrection of the old Holy Roman Empire—to correct His sinning people.

This strong and deadly leader's mind will *change* and become far more evil (Habakkuk 1:11; Isaiah 10:7). He is going to *martyr God's people* ("the holy people")—those who have rebelled against God. Other prophecies show that this martyrdom will occur during a time Jesus Christ calls "great tribulation" (Matthew 24:21; Revelation 6:9-11). They also reveal that the end-time nations of Israel (America and Britain) will be conquered during the same period (e.g. Isaiah 10:5-6; Jeremiah 1:13-14; 30:4-7).* This tyrant wants to "blot out the name of Israel."

So Daniel 8:24 applies to spiritual Israel (God's Church) *and* prophetic Israel (America and Britain). *Both will be corrected at the same time and by the same European power.* Barack Obama has led and is still leading Biden and America to their death (Ezekiel 33:11). He is destroying America, and everybody should see that. He has played a key role in weakening the U.S. to the point that the Holy Roman Empire can easily conquer us.

The nations of Israel also "cast down the truth to the ground" (Daniel 8:12) in a secular way. The U.S. superpower leads the charge. Its Constitution, which is based on many biblical principles, is being assailed and scrapped. This nation also rejected God's warning message, as did Britain. The *context* of Daniel 8 shows us this.

"And through his policy also he shall cause craft to prosper in

---

* This is all explained and proved from Scripture in our free book *The United States and Britain in Prophecy.*

his hand; and he shall magnify himself in his heart, and by peace shall destroy many ..." (verse 25). Notice: This Antiochus has a policy of craft. He *misleads people,* appearing to come in peace before he destroys them!

This is the way Satan operates. To destroy God's Church, he managed to plant a *spiritual* Antiochus right at the top, who desecrated the spiritual temple and cast the truth to the ground. And to destroy the nations of Israel, Satan will use a *political* Antiochus who leads the end-time European empire. His army will march right into the Holy City, Jerusalem, to begin his physical assault (e.g. Daniel 11:31; Mark 13:14; Luke 21:20). The United States, Britain and Israel (biblical Judah) are all prophesied to fall together at the hands of that European power (Hosea 5:5).

Biblical prophecy shows that Satan leads both the first spiritual Antiochus and this last political Antiochus (who leads the European empire). We now know that HE USED THE SAME STRATEGY TO WEAKEN PHYSICAL ISRAEL IN BETWEEN THOSE TWO ATTACKS. The highest office in the world's number one superpower, which happens to be a descendant of ancient Israel, is a big target for Satan. There he placed *another Antiochus-type* who undermines the nations of Israel and prepares them for their destruction by a united Europe!

This is why we can apply the Daniel 8 prophecy to prophetic Israel. This chapter has a *duality* that helps us understand verses 9-12. The key of duality unlocks many Bible prophecies. *Sadly, the tragedy and devastation within God's Church is now playing out on a grand scale in America and Britain.* The Great Tribulation is approaching rapidly.

This Tribulation period—during which God, as punishment for these peoples, allows Satan and the demons devastating power—lasts 2½ years. Then comes the Day of the Lord, when God Himself will correct those who still refuse to repent. This will last one year, for a total of 3½ years (Revelation 11:2-3; 13:5).

Then, thankfully, will come the Second Coming of Jesus Christ, which will bring an end to all the suffering! (Daniel 8:25).

A 'MAN OF SIN'

Another prophecy provides still more detail relevant to what is happening in America today.

In 2 Thessalonians 2, the Apostle Paul prophesied about some events that would occur just before "the coming of our Lord Jesus Christ" (verse 1). Notice this astounding prophecy: "Let no man deceive you by any means: for that day [the Second Coming of Christ] shall not come, except there come *a falling away first, and that man of sin be revealed, the son of perdition* [or *destruction*]" (verse 3). This is a great "falling away" in the Church. When Satan attacked God's Church, it triggered a GREAT FALLING AWAY because most of God's people were lukewarm, and God's work was destroyed.

This prophecy says a "man of sin" would be revealed *inside that Church.* This man is called the "son of perdition," or destruction"—the same title as Judas Iscariot, who was actually POSSESSED BY THE DEVIL (Luke 22:3; John 13:27). Satan has a lot of power. And SATAN USED A MAN.

This man "opposeth and exalteth himself above all that is called God, or that is worshipped; so that he as God sitteth in the temple of God, shewing himself that he is God" (2 Thessalonians 2:4). This Satan-inspired man acted like he was God, taking the place of God in that spiritual temple. That is how arrogant Satan is, acting like God. He thinks he is God, and he has rebelled against God and tried to *overthrow* God! And he inspired a "man of sin" who did the same.

The prophecy in 2 Thessalonians 2 also includes another important individual.

Verse 7 speaks of a man who "restrained" this evil force in the Church until he was taken out of the way (Revised Standard Version). That man was Herbert W. Armstrong. After he died in 1986, the devil was cast down and this "man of sin," also called the "son of perdition," took over the Church.* Using this man, Satan

---

* Read more about this in Appendix B: "The Devil Cast Down."

was able to destroy the Church that Mr. Armstrong had founded.

And notice what happened immediately after that: "And THEN SHALL THAT WICKED [Satan the devil] BE REVEALED, whom the Lord shall consume with the spirit of his mouth, and shall destroy with the brightness of his coming" (verse 8). *After* Mr. Armstrong was taken out of the way, Satan was cast down (see Appendix B). Now everybody can see him because he is full of wrath and wreaking great destruction! Satan turned 95 percent of the people in God's Church away from God. God had to raise up another work through the 5 percent who remained faithful to the truth, to REVEAL Satan and his man to those who are willing to see. God would not allow this spiritual Antiochus to blot out the name of Israel, but he did wreck most of God's Church!

Verse 9 says this man comes "after the working of Satan with all power and signs and lying wonders." Can you detect this evil spiritual influence in our world today? It is a real spiritual power, and it practically mesmerizes people with its lies! This points back to Revelation 12:9 and the fact that Satan has unmatched powers of deception.

WHAT HAPPENED IN GOD'S CHURCH SHOWS YOU SOMETHING OF A BLUEPRINT FOR WHAT SATAN BEGAN TO DO IN THESE NATIONS. This is why that Church history is so relevant and important for you to grasp.

The book you are reading exposes the devil. We saw firsthand what he did to the Church. Now we are watching him unleash the same kind of destruction on our nations! The difference is, the destruction in God's Church was on a spiritual level, and the three nations are being destroyed *physically.* This will lead to these nations being *conquered* by a Satan-possessed leader (Hosea 5:5; Habakkuk 1:11).

These scriptures reveal one of the defining spiritual truths of our world today. They explain why America is rapidly being transformed into a different nation!

WHAT INVALUABLE INSIGHT BIBLICAL PROPHECY AND PROPHETIC DUALITY GIVE US.

APPENDIX B

THE DEVIL CAST DOWN

T HERE IS A REASON WORLD EVENTS HAVE TAKEN SUCH A DARK, inexplicable turn in recent years. The Bible reveals that reason and when it began.

Note closely this stunning prophecy in Revelation 12: "And there was war in heaven: Michael and his angels fought against the dragon; and the dragon fought and his angels, And prevailed not; neither was their place found any more in heaven. And the great dragon was cast out, that old serpent, called the Devil, and Satan, which deceiveth the whole world: he was cast out into the earth, and his angels were cast out with him. ... Therefore rejoice, ye heavens, and ye that dwell in them. Woe to the inhabiters of the earth and of the sea! for the devil is come down unto you, having great wrath, because he knoweth that he hath but a short time" (verses 7-9, 12).

These are crucial verses. They describe WAR IN HEAVEN between Satan and God.

Lucifer was one of only three archangels mentioned in the Bible, the highest of all the angels God created. He worked directly at God's throne (see Isaiah 14 and Ezekiel 28). But he allowed selfishness and arrogance to enter his mind and became Satan. He influenced millions of angels to think this same way, and he led a massive rebellion against God. There was war in heaven, and God struck him down from heaven "as lightning" (Luke 10:18).

Then God began a new plan through mankind. Satan used his great power to attack the minds of the very first human beings,

Adam and Eve, and draw them into sin. He has influenced and deceived all their descendants ever since (see Ephesians 2:2; 2 Corinthians 4:4; Revelation 12:9).

But Satan still had access to the whole universe and to God (e.g. Job 1:6). Revelation 12:7-12 describe *another* war in heaven that occurred much later. Satan warred against God, and God cast him and the millions of demons to Earth—AND CONFINED THEM HERE IN THIS END TIME!

Now this Earth is infested with millions of demons—led by the devil!

That meant far more trouble for this Earth: "WOE TO THE INHABITERS OF THE EARTH AND OF THE SEA!" (verse 12). Satan and the demons hate God and His plan for His human creation. As horrible as their influence has been throughout human history, the destruction they are now unleashing on the world is unprecedented!

Satan is brimming with "GREAT WRATH"! He is in a foaming fit of rage. Why? "[B]ecause he knoweth that he hath but a short time" (verse 12). He has nothing to lose. Since that gigantic turning point when Satan was cast down, the devil's time has grown shorter and shorter, his anger has gotten worse and worse, and his power and wicked influence have grown far stronger. This Earth has never experienced the full wrath of Satan UNTIL THIS END TIME.

Revelation 20:1-3 and other Bible prophecies show that Satan's "short time" will terminate at the return of Jesus Christ, when he will be banished *even from Earth* and imprisoned in a bottomless pit. When God cast Satan down from heaven to Earth the first time, he did *not* have "but a short time"!

This shows that Revelation 12:7-12 is an *end-time* prophecy.

Since the time of Satan and the demons' internment here, the world has grown far more dangerous, immoral and lawless. These wicked beings have targeted, attacked, corrupted and destroyed exactly the things that the Bible reveals are essential to God's plan for man: God's laws, God's Church, God's nations and God's institutions of family, sex and morality, which reveal the incredible reason God created human beings. This wicked influence is destroying human minds and preparing to murder *billions* of human lives in a global holocaust!

This change has deeply affected the United States. In fact, it marked a major escalation of a violent attack on America. This malevolent spiritual army, though invisible, is very real and deadly dangerous.

To understand events in America and the rest of the world in this end time, we must understand this. Even most Christians know nothing about it, yet it *has happened*—in our day. Many scriptures corroborate this.

Satan was cast down at a *specific time*. WHEN did this occur? As improbable as it may sound, an overwhelming amount of evidence shows that this prophecy was fulfilled at a definite time in recent history.

SATAN'S FIRST TARGET

For clues as to when this war took place, let's ask: After the devil attacked God and God constrained him to Earth, where did he go? What was his first target? What then was his second target? The answers to these questions reveal a great deal about God and the devil.

Revelation 12:13 reveals the *first* target of Satan's raging wrath: "And when the dragon saw that he was cast unto the earth, he *persecuted the woman* which brought forth the man child." The woman in this passage, described in more detail in verses 1-2, symbolizes the Church of God.

Jesus Christ personally raised up the one true Church of God and said it would remain through seven successive eras until His return (see Matthew 16:18 and Revelation 2-3). The true Church of God does, in fact, exist! In this end time, it was led by Herbert W. Armstrong. Under his leadership, God restored the true Christian doctrines to the Church. That Church did a powerful global work. It possessed and proclaimed the truths of the Bible on a weekly broadcast on more than 400 television stations, in a newsmagazine with over 8 million subscribers, at three colleges and through many more superb initiatives.

Yet tragically, within a few years after Mr. Armstrong died, that Church and its work were destroyed! The doctrines were changed; the truth was cast down; the various projects were scaled back, undermined or canceled.*

That destruction is powerful evidence of an unprecedented satanic attack. WHEN MILLIONS OF DEMONS ASSAULT ONE LITTLE FLOCK, YOU ARE SURE TO SEE STARTLING EFFECTS. EVEN THE WORLD COULD SEE THE ENORMOUS DISASTER! The sudden, catastrophic, nearly complete destruction of the true Church, starting with its principles and beliefs, reveals that Satan and millions of demons directed their rage at God's Church. Within just a few short years, it was spiritually destroyed, and THE GREAT MAJORITY OF GOD'S PEOPLE WERE CONQUERED BY THE DEVIL. You really cannot explain what happened to that Church any other way.

That gives you a sense of the *power* these evil spirit beings have. Without God's protection, we stand no chance against them!

One truth that Mr. Armstrong had restored was the understanding of Israel and the name of Israel (Matthew 17:11). Only the true Church, spiritual Israel, has that truth. When 2 Kings 14:27 speaks of someone trying to "blot out the name of Israel from under heaven," or all over this Earth, the Church—which has the real understanding of the name of Israel—is the first target! When Mr. Armstrong died and Satan and millions of demons were cast down and confined to Earth, they attacked the only people who understood and proclaimed the name of Israel to the world! A spiritual Antiochus got control of God's true Church and cast the truth to the ground—but he could *not* blot out the name of Israel.

---

* You can read more about this Church in Appendix A: "Prophetic Duality." To learn what happened in detail, request your free copy of our book *Raising the Ruins.*

Verse 13 of Revelation 12 specifically dates this prophecy. We can point to a *specific time* when God's true Church was forcibly attacked by the devil. It strongly appears all this began immediately after Mr. Armstrong died on January 16, 1986.*

Verses 14-16 show how Satan will continue attacking the Church right up to the beginning of the Great Tribulation. This refers to the final, violent climax of Satan-deceived human civilization. It will last 3½ years ("a time, and times, and half a time"; see also Matthew 24:21; Revelation 11:2 and 13:5, which describe the same time period as 42 months; and Revelation 11:3, which describes it as 1,260 days). Revelation 12:14 says the Church will be protected in a place of safety during that nightmarish period. But it is speaking of those *few* who remained *faithful* to God and did *not* cast His truth to the ground. This little remnant kept Satan from blotting out the name of Israel! These people are rewarded physically and spiritually for proclaiming God's warning message to this world. This is why God protects them from the greatest suffering ever on Earth.

SATAN HOPED TO BLOT OUT THE NAME OF ISRAEL. BUT GOD WILL NEVER ALLOW THAT. God is going to protect His faithful people who guard the name of Israel. Nobody guards this name more than spiritual Israel, God's true Church.

Yet the *great majority* of God's people turned from God and allowed Satan to conquer them. They will experience Satan's wrath in the Tribulation (verse 17).

This all establishes the time frame: Satan was cast down in the end time, shortly before the Tribulation. He knows his time is short, so he is moving like lightning to destroy. His first target was the Church of God, and the recent history of that Church shows the woeful results of his great wrath.

What, then, was the devil's next target?

---

* This is fully explained in *Malachi's Message* and *Raising the Ruins*. All of our literature is free.

SATAN'S SECOND TARGET

The end-time Great Tribulation described in Revelation 12:14-17 is discussed in many Bible prophecies. They show that the primary target of Satan's great wrath is Israel. The Church of God is spiritual Israel, and the nations that descended from the ancient Israelites are physical Israel. These nations are the United States, Britain, the Jewish nation and a number of related English-speaking nations. Throughout history, God has used Israel and the nations that descended from it. Satan is focused on bringing them down.

In America, Satan has particularly attacked the principles, beliefs and history connecting our people back to the Bible and to God. Just as he destroyed the truth in spiritual Israel, he is destroying the truth about history, morality, race, sex and family in America and the other nations of Israel. By doing this, Satan has also been able to besiege the government, media, economy and military. These institutions have deteriorated *rapidly* since Satan was cast down. This puts the whole world in greater danger.

This world has changed dramatically since Herbert W. Armstrong died. Everything indicates that Satan was cast down around that time. That event marked a turning point in history. Now this world is on a downhill plunge to destruction! Evil and dreadful events are unfolding as never before. A vicious spirit is clearly at work.

Note the chronology: After the devil attacked the Church in verse 13 and devastated it and destroyed the people's faith, he continues his destructive rampage on a larger scale until God has to take His faithful people to a place of safety. That also tells you that the devil is attacking three nations of Israel—America the superpower and the British peoples (prophetic Israel—the birthright nations) and biblical Judah (the scepter nation: Genesis 49:10). These nations have been blessed far more than the other Israelite nations. That is why God is punishing them more. The part of that attack that *precedes* the Great Tribulation is not specifically explained here, but it is in other scriptures.

America has been *under attack.* These prophecies reveal why.

DEMONIZING ROBERT BORK

One prominent national event that revealed the start of Satan's destruction was the vicious lawlessness that was unleashed during the confirmation hearings of Robert Bork in 1987. President Ronald Reagan had nominated Bork to become an associate justice on the United States Supreme Court. He was a great defender of the Constitution and the law. Yet just 45 minutes into the confirmation hearing, Massachusetts Democrat Edward Kennedy took to the Senate floor and brazenly demonized him. "Robert Bork's America," he said, would produce back-alley abortions, segregation, censorship and midnight police raids.

It was a shocking, dishonest vilification of a man who was obviously qualified and greatly respected, even by many liberals. "There was not a line in that speech that was accurate," Bork said. Many people agreed—*but the attack still worked.* Senator Kennedy and others led the way for abortionists, evolutionists, feminists, civil-rights advocates and other liberals to band together and defame Judge Bork's reputation in an enormous smear campaign. They even aired television ads denigrating him. "They turned him into an absolute gargoyle, into a beast," one senator said. The liberal *Washington Post* admitted that it was a "lynching." Many other liberals saw what was happening too. The head of the Senate Judiciary Committee was Joe Biden, and he said he didn't believe they could reject a man of Bork's qualifications. But special interest groups caused him to join the attack.

Why was Robert Bork so demonized? The reason was that the radical left *feared* him.

Judge Bork was known for one thing more than anything else: believing in the Constitution. He was one of the most brilliant constitutional lawyers this land has produced. He was considered "a pioneer in constitutional thinking devoted to the text and original meaning of the Constitution," as Reuters put it. He was known as a constitutional originalist or constructionist who believed in judicial restraint.

That is why the left hated him. THE CONSTITUTION IS THE

SUPREME LAW OF THE LAND. MUCH OF IT IS BASED ON BIBLICAL PRINCIPLES. The attack against the Constitution radically intensified in the mid-1980s, and it accelerated America's descent into deadly, anti-God lawlessness.

Everyone had thought that when a popular president nominated a brilliant, well-qualified, passionately pro-Constitution judge to a court whose purpose is to protect the Constitution, he would be easily confirmed, even by a majority Democrat Senate. But in 1987, radical liberals despised the Constitution, and they were openly hostile enough and powerful enough to get their way. The Senate defeated Judge Bork's nomination 58 to 42, the largest margin ever.

MANY PEOPLE AT THE TIME RECOGNIZED THAT THIS WAS A MAJOR TURNING POINT IN AMERICAN POLITICS. One law professor said it was "the decisive moment in politicizing the process of judicial selection" that "poisoned the atmosphere for judicial confirmations ever since." In fact, it poisoned far more than that!

The tide turned in a big way in 1987. Law started to get a lot weaker. And lawlessness started to grow much, much stronger. SUCH A MASSIVE LURCH TOWARD LAWLESSNESS HAS A CAUSE. THIS PROPHECY IN REVELATION 12 REVEALS THAT CAUSE.

EFFECTS ON SOCIETY

So many of the evils plaguing America today trace back to the mid-1980s. Consider just a few examples.

Today, many people recognize the immense threat posed by illegal immigration and the fact that radical leftists are actively using it to weaken the country. This demographic transformation of the country's population has been underway for more than a generation. In fact, IT BEGAN WITH THE 1986 IMMIGRATION REFORM AND CONTROL ACT, WHICH GRANTED AMNESTY TO MILLIONS OF ILLEGAL IMMIGRANTS AND LIBERALIZED AMERICA'S IMMIGRATION LAWS.

Mass shootings have become tragically commonplace in

America. This is a horrific sign of heavy demonic influence if not possession! One database shows that there were fewer than five mass shootings per year in the United States until about 1988, when the number of such incidents began to notably increase. NOW MORE THAN 40 MASS SHOOTINGS OCCUR EVERY YEAR—ABOUT ONE EVERY NINE DAYS.

Mental illness was ranked among the top five conditions accounting for rising health-care costs between 1987 and 2000. The United States government approved fluoxetine for medical use in December 1987, and pharmaceutical companies began marketing drugs like Prozac to "cure" depression. Prozac sales soared, but so did the number of depressed people. Today, nearly a quarter of Americans are taking powerful prescription drugs to try to improve mental health, and mental illnesses are worse than ever! Analysts have noted that a number of mass shooters have been on Prozac prescriptions.

IN 1986, DRUG CARTELS OPENED UP NEW DRUG "PIPELINES" BETWEEN COLOMBIA'S COCAINE FIELDS AND AMERICA'S INNER CITIES. Cocaine-related hospital emergencies rose 110 percent. Drug use in America has expanded massively, and many states have even legalized certain drugs. BEFORE 1986, SUCH A DRUGGED STATE OF OUR COUNTRY WOULD HAVE BEEN UNBELIEVABLE!

Around this same time, video-game developers began working on an infamous video game featuring lifelike, realistic violence designed for teenaged consumption. Today, video games, including numerous realistic first-person shooters (often preferred by mass shooters), are an enormous industry—even more lucrative than our blood- and sex-soaked movie industry.

While our movies became more and more wicked, so too did music such as heavy metal and even more mainstream genres. An increasingly popular and even glamorized subject for our entertainment industry today is *suicide*. Satanic-related fashions became more and more popular, as did outright occultism and even satanic ritual abuse. Many religious people have suspected that something dramatic changed in the 1980s.

Our lurch toward lawlessness and evil can be traced back to a turning point in the mid-1980s. That is because Satan and his demons were cast down at that time and thereafter intensified their attack on America. Elites are now actively destroying the Constitution and undermining law enforcement. They are denigrating anything godly and good about American history. They are applauding and elevating the wicked and unjust. They are intentionally exacerbating social divisions. They are destroying the family, even attacking the very existence of male and female! These are Satan-inspired attacks that highlight the heightened influence of this evil spiritual force.

A THREE-PRONGED ATTACK

Biblical prophecy shows that after Satan was cast down, he retaliated with a three-pronged attack. First, he attacked God's Church, spiritual Israel. Second, he attacked three nations of prophetic Israel in this end time, especially the lead nation, the United States. Third, he will work through the soon-to-be-resurrected Holy Roman Empire to destroy these nations militarily. That is Satan's master plan for destroying spiritual and physical Israel—BUT THEY STILL HAVE ONE LAST CHANCE TO REPENT *BEFORE* THE GREAT TRIBULATION! (Amos 7:8).

Looking at these prophecies and viewing actual end-time events, it is clear the devil uses an Antiochus-type in all three phases.

The first of these end-time types of Antiochus became the head of God's Church. The second was a political Antiochus who became America's president. Third, Satan will use the head of a resurrected Holy Roman Empire to attack America and Britain.

All three of these Antiochus-type men work from within (one as a "lover"—Ezekiel 23) to do their destructive work. DANIEL 8 SHOWS HOW SATAN CONTROLS ALL THREE OF THESE MEN.

ALSO, ALL THREE TRY TO "BLOT OUT THE NAME OF ISRAEL" physically and spiritually. Satan wants to totally blot out that name, which represents God's master plan for all mankind who has ever lived. Every person who enters God's Kingdom, or Family, will have to learn and accept the name of Israel. All mankind will become spiritual Israel, which will be full of abundant prosperity, freedom and joy forever.

BUT A SHORT TIME

America and the other modern nations of Israel are under vicious attack. We are losing the principles and blessings that made our nations great. We must remember that our peoples did not create those principles or those blessings: Those things came *from God,* for the benefit not just of the modern nations of Israel but for all mankind! That is why Satan hates them and is attacking them. And, because our people have forgotten God, He is allowing Satan to wreak terrible destruction on physical Israel, just as He allowed him to destroy spiritual Israel.

This is terrible news. But intertwined with this tragic truth is the best news you could possibly hear! That is because Satan's attack proves not only these prophecies about God's true Church and about the nations of Israel, but also the prophecy of Revelation 12:12 that *he has but a short time.* Satan was cast down in 1986, and now he has even less time before his window of opportunity closes. His throne on Earth is about to be *taken away* at the return of Jesus Christ! And many Bible prophecies show that His return is coming soon. Jesus Christ is going to rule Earth from *His* throne!

Satan's intensifying attack is about to erupt into mass bloodshed so violent and widespread that it is impossible to imagine. This Great Tribulation is *mainly* the result of Satan's great wrath. But there is a good reason he is so full of wrath. What causes *him* great wrath should cause *us* great *joy.* Satan's attack against God's Church and against the nations of Israel is his *last* attack before Jesus Christ returns!

WAS THE CORONAVIRUS CRISIS ENGINEERED?

C OVID-19 TURNED OUR WORLD ON ITS HEAD. IT ENABLED unprecedented government oppression worldwide. Where did this virus come from? We do not yet know everything there is to know, but its murky origins are becoming clearer. The emerging picture makes an absolutely incredible scenario look more and more plausible: *that American leaders contributed to engineering COVID-19 as a bioweapon for "fundamentally transforming" America.*

BIOLAB NETWORK

When in 1991 it became clear to American leaders that the Soviet Union was about to collapse, the George H.W. Bush administration began to worry about Soviet weapons falling into the wrong hands. Senators Sam Nunn and Richard Lugar established the Cooperative Threat Reduction program, which provided funding and expertise for former Soviet states to decommission biological, chemical and nuclear weapons stockpiles. Yet 14 years after this program started, Senators Lugar and Barack Obama decided that the U.S. should start *managing* former Soviet biological weapons programs, instead of shutting them down.

In 2005, Lugar and Obama met with Ukrainian leaders and signed an agreement under which the U.S. Department of Defense promised to assist the Ukrainian Ministry of Health in ensuring that Ukrainian biolabs were never used to develop bioweapons. This agreement opened the door for the U.S. Defense Threat Reduction Agency to award Kansas-based construction company Black & Veatch with millions of dollars to build a level-3 biosecurity lab in Odessa, Ukraine. Although this was the first biolab to be constructed in Ukraine under the Nunn-Lugar Global Cooperative Threat Reduction Program, it was not the last. A Defense Department factsheet released on March 11, 2022, reveals that the Pentagon had invested at least $200 million supporting Ukrainian 46 laboratories, health facilities and diagnostic sites.

Understanding this biolab network is key to understanding how COVID-19 originated.

The Bulletin of the Atomic Scientists has confirmed that 336 facilities in 30 different countries have received funding from the U.S. Biological Threat Reduction Program, and one of this program's key partners in Ukraine is the San Francisco-based medical data firm Metabiota.

In 2014, Metabiota received $23.9 million from the U.S. Department of Defense, just two months after it received $500,000 from Hunter Biden's investment firm Rosemont Seneca Partners LLC. We know from e-mails on the now infamous Hunter Biden laptop that Metabiota was working on a special "science project" involving Ukrainian biolabs with the gas company Burisma Holdings LLC (where Hunter held a position on the board of directors).

We do not know much more about this shady "science project" because President Trump was impeached for suggesting that the Ukrainian government investigate Biden family business dealings in Ukraine. But we do know that Metabiota founder Dr. Nathan Wolfe coauthored a study on bat coronaviruses in 2017 with EcoHealth president Dr. Peter Daszak. And we know that Dr. Wolfe has also served on the EcoHealth Alliance's editorial board since 2004.

We will see as we go along that Dr. Daszak and EcoHealth Alliance were intricately involved in the biological research that produced the SARS-CoV-2. And it is important to realize that both Metabiota and EcoHealth alliance began receiving funding from the Pentagon's Defense Threat Reduction Agency during President Obama's second term. The Obama administration claimed this money was to ensure foreign labs were not engaging in bioweapons research. But the truth is that BY OUTSOURCING WORK TO PRIVATE COMPANIES WORKING IN FOREIGN COUNTRIES, THE U.S. THREAT REDUCTION AGENCY WAS ABLE TO CIRCUMVENT CONGRESSIONAL OVERSIGHT.

THE WUHAN LAB

A year before Senators Lugar and Obama made their 2005 trip to Ukraine, the Jean Mérieux Laboratory in France began a joint project with the Chinese Academy of Sciences to build a level-4 biosecurity lab in Wuhan, China. This lab took 11 years and $44 million to build, eventually becoming the now infamous Wuhan Institute of Virology. This lab was completed on January 31, 2015. Yet the scandals began long before it was finished.

In a leaked U.S. State Department cable from 2009, Secretary of State Hillary Clinton warned 40 American allies that research at this laboratory could lead to bioterrorism. Yet the French continued collaborating with Communist China—until the Communists kicked them out of the lab in 2017. Other State Department cables show that the Wuhan lab began conducting classified research for the Chinese military at about that time.

According to investigative journalist Sharri Markson, the State Department obtained a book authored by 18 Chinese scientists and public health bureaucrats in 2015 that described severe acute respiratory syndrome coronaviruses as part of a "new era of genetic weapons." This volume was titled *The Unnatural Origins of SARS and New Species of Man-made Viruses as Genetic Weapons*. It notes that CORONAVIRUSES CAN BE "ARTIFICIALLY

MANIPULATED INTO AN EMERGING HUMAN DISEASE VIRUS, THEN WEAPONIZED AND UNLEASHED IN A WAY NEVER SEEN BEFORE."*

THIS BOOK FURTHER REVEALED THAT CHINESE SCIENTISTS HAVE BEEN PREPARING FOR A WORLD WAR FOUGHT NOT WITH ATOMIC WEAPONS BUT BIOLOGICAL AND GENETIC WEAPONS. Referencing how the two atomic bombs dropped on Japan during World War II forced them to surrender, the authors claim bioweapons will be "the core weapon for victory" in a third world war.

Former State Department official David Asher told the *Daily Caller* that leading French officials warned the State Department that they had grave concerns about what kind of research was being done at the Wuhan Institute of Virology around the time this book was released in 2015. So PRESIDENT BARACK OBAMA HAD ACCESS TO ENOUGH INTELLIGENCE TO KNOW THE DANGERS OF COLLABORATING WITH THE CHINESE ON GENETIC RESEARCH—YET HE WAS MOTIVATED TO COLLABORATE NONETHELESS.

According to Dr. Andrew Huff, a former vice president of EcoHealth Alliance, the Wuhan Institute of Virology started collaborating with EcoHealth in 2009, the very year Hillary Clinton warned that research at this laboratory could lead to bioterrorism. Yet rather than step in and stop EcoHealth Alliance from engaging in such dangerous research, the Defense Threat Reduction Agency gave EcoHealth Alliance $37.6 million for biomedical research. This funding started in 2013 and included $6.5 million for studying bat-borne diseases in West Asia.

In his book *The Truth About Wuhan: How I Uncovered the Biggest Lie in History,* Dr. Huff revealed that EcoHealth Alliance was not using the money the Defense Threat Reduction Agency gave it to stop bioweapons development. Rather, it was actually teaching the Wuhan Institute of Virology the best existing methods to engineer bat coronaviruses to attack other species.

---

* These Chinese scientists believed SARS-CoV-1 was a bioweapon engineered in the United States; so it is possible some of them helped engineer SARS-CoV-2 as an act of revenge.

This was a shocking turn of events. A government office founded to keep Soviet technology out of the wrong hands was instead spreading that technology to other nations.

Dr. Huff resigned from EcoHealth Alliance in 2016 when he found out that the company was not merely studying existing viruses but was also creating monstrous new viruses. "I was terrified by what I saw," he said in a Sun Online interview. "WE WERE JUST HANDING THEM BIOWEAPON TECHNOLOGY."

EcoHealth Alliance was also receiving funds from the CIA-backed venture capital firm In-Q-Tel, so both Barack Obama and his spymaster John Brennan must have known what EcoHealth was doing. Yet they allowed this firm to continue its dangerous work.

WHY WOULD OBAMA GIVE SO MUCH MONEY TO A CHINESE LAB SUSPECTED OF BIOTERRORISM? EVEN HILLARY CLINTON KNEW IT WAS DANGEROUS, SO THE ANSWER MIGHT BE MORE SINISTER THAN YOU THINK.

RADICAL ENVIRONMENTALIST

Barack Obama's science czar, Dr. John P. Holdren, was one of his more radical appointees. This man has written extensively on global environmental change. In 1973, Holdren encouraged a decline in fertility to well below replacement in the U.S. because "210 million now is too many and 280 million in 2040 is likely to be much too many." He has called for a global regime to enforce population limits. He has advocated population control measures such as mandatory abortions, sterilization after a second child, or sterilants put in the drinking water. This sounds like something out of a dystopian novel, but Holdren says it is necessary to reduce stresses on the environment. And Obama chose him as director of the Office of Science and Technology.

What kind of research was Holdren doing for Obama?

On July 5, 2016, *Nature* magazine published an interview with Dr. Holdren, in which he said, "I'm going to China this week for a strategic and economic dialogue and for a U.S.-China dialogue on innovation policy. ... We have a lot of cooperation with China on biomedical issues. We talk to them all of the time about gain-of-function research and about gene-editing issues."

HOLDREN WAS COLLABORATING WITH THE CHINESE TO MAKE VIRUSES MORE DEADLY!

This collaboration is even more concerning since it occurred after Obama suspended funding for gain-of-function research in America on October 17, 2014, due to fears that such experiments could *cause a pandemic.* Yet it allowed an exception to this funding ban if "the research is urgently necessary to protect the public health or national security." The U.S. military took advantage of this exception and continued funding research at the Wuhan Institute of Virology, which held a collection of coronaviruses. Dr. Huff believes that lack of effective oversight allowed certain members of the U.S. government to outsource gain-of-function research to overseas labs while such research was banned domestically. But when you dig into the background of some of Obama's top appointees, it seems clear that OBAMA, HOLDREN AND THEIR STAFF TRUSTED COMMUNIST CHINA MORE THAN THEY TRUSTED U.S. RESEARCHERS!

Congress cannot investigate Metabiota activity in Ukraine or EcoHealth Alliance activity in China like they can investigate domestic biolab research, so pausing gain-of-function research domestically while continuing it internationally is a great way to continue bioweapons research you do not want the American people to find out about. And EVERY INDICATION IS THAT OBAMA DID NOT WANT THE AMERICAN PEOPLE TO KNOW ABOUT WHAT WAS REALLY GOING ON IN HIS OVERSEAS BIOLABS.

FUNDING COMMUNISTS

Congressman Guy Reschenthaler uncovered $1.1 million in Obama-era taxpayer funding funneled to the Wuhan Institute of Virology through EcoHealth Alliance for gain-of-function research.

The goal was to create a man-made virus by inserting a spiked protein from a wild bat coronavirus into a mouse-adapted SARS-CoV backbone. The U.S. Agency for International Development awarded this funding, adding to the nearly $600,000 sent to Wuhan from the National Institute of Allergy and Infectious Diseases, which is run by DR. ANTHONY FAUCI. (We don't yet know how much of the $37.6 million that the Defense Threat Reduction Agency gave to EcoHealth Alliance funneled down to the Wuhan Institute of Virology, but Dr. Huff indicates in his book that EcoHealth Alliance relied on the U.S. Agency for International Development to fund the actual gain-of-function research while using Pentagon money for other projects.)

The main point is that DR. FAUCI CLEARLY KNEW ABOUT THE DANGEROUS GENETICS RESEARCH BEING DONE IN WUHAN. He calls it gain-of-function research, but THAT IS JUST A TECHNICAL TITLE FOR BIOWEAPONS RESEARCH. HE WAS MAKING MOUSE AND BAT CORONAVIRUSES MORE DEADLY TO HUMAN BEINGS, AND HE DISGUISED IT AS VACCINE RESEARCH.

Speaking at the 2017 Consortium of Universities for Global Health conference, Dr. Daszak admitted that his controversial "work on coronaviruses in China" was carried out with funding from the U.S. Agency for International Development Emerging Pandemic Threats program and Fauci's National Institutes of Health agency. The four major partners in the U.S. Agency for International Development Emerging Pandemic Threats program are EcoHealth Alliance, Metabiota, the Smithsonian Institute and the Wildlife Conservation Society. So the people in charge of the U.S.-run Ukrainian biolabs knew about what was going on in Wuhan as well. As mentioned earlier, Dr. Wolfe even collaborated with Daszak on some bat research that year.

Some scientists were understandably concerned about this funding. The U.S. government's National Science Advisory Board for Biosecurity studied whether research should continue into enhancing "potential pandemic pathogens." IN 2016, IT REPORTED THAT THOUGH SUCH RESEARCH COULD BENEFIT PUBLIC HEALTH, IT

ALSO ENTAILED SIGNIFICANT RISKS. THE BOARD RECOMMENDED ADDITIONAL SCRUTINY. PRESIDENT OBAMA IGNORED THIS RECOMMENDATION.

In November 2016, the federal government establishment was rocked by the unexpected election of Donald Trump as president. This victory came in spite of the fact that Obama, his "deep state" collaborators and the propaganda media worked—even illegally—to sabotage the Trump campaign and, after the election, the Trump transition team.

Eleven days before Trump took office, Obama *reauthorized* the type of gain-of-function research he had banned in 2014 and resumed funding for creating SARS coronavirus biological weapons. The authorization stated that researchers who followed federal guidelines "will satisfy the requirements for lifting the current moratorium on certain life sciences research that could enhance a pathogen's virulence and/or transmissibility to produce a potential pandemic pathogen."

How ominous this is to read, knowing what a pandemic pathogen, and government reactions to it, would produce before the 2020 presidential election.

Investigative journalist Mark Bradman noted, "[E]ssentially this reauthorization was only kick-starting funding within the U.S. because the funding of weaponization of SARS-CoV-2 never actually stopped in 2014" (Conservative Treehouse, June 5, 2021). Obama's order did not affect the type of research going on in China, but it allowed academics like Dr. Ralph Baric at the University of North Carolina to collaborate with their Wuhan counterparts more effectively.

DANGEROUS COLLABORATION

THE DAY AFTER OBAMA REAUTHORIZED GAIN-OF-FUNCTION RESEARCH, DR. FAUCI GAVE A SPEECH AT GEORGETOWN UNIVERSITY ABOUT PANDEMIC PREPAREDNESS. In it, he basically predicted the COVID-19 pandemic. "No matter what, history has told us definitively that [outbreaks] will happen, because [facing] infectious diseases is a perpetual challenge," he said. "THE THING WE'RE EXTRAORDINARILY CONFIDENT ABOUT IS THAT WE'RE GOING TO SEE THIS IN THE NEXT FEW YEARS."

Dr. Fauci was funding gain-of-function research in China while simultaneously warning the American people to brace for a pandemic. He never mentioned he was involved in the dangerous manipulation of bat coronaviruses to produce a potential pandemic pathogen, but he seemed to know that the world was heading into a serious infectious disease crisis. THE FACT THAT HE SAID THIS A DAY AFTER OBAMA REAUTHORIZED BIOWEAPONS RESEARCH MAKES IT EVEN MORE SUSPICIOUS.

Markson told Steve Bannon on his *War Room* podcast that most of the scientific community thought gain-of-function experimentation with deadly viruses was too dangerous; so to keep it moving forward, Dr. Fauci had to argue against scientific consensus. Then she recounted that Dr. Fauci used President Obama's reauthorization to restart this research in 2017 after Donald Trump took office. *So most of the scientific community was against doing gain-of-function research,* but DR. FAUCI ENSURED THIS RESEARCH CONTINUED DURING THE TRUMP ADMINISTRATION.

ALL THE EVIDENCE SUGGESTS COVID-19 ORIGINATED IN A LAB THAT THE SCIENTIFIC COMMUNITY WANTED NOTHING TO DO WITH UNTIL BARACK OBAMA, JOHN HOLDREN AND ANTHONY FAUCI FORCED THEIR WILL ON EVERYONE ELSE! What was it that made this worth it? *What was their agenda?*

OBAMA'S MOTIVE

Why would Barack Obama reauthorize funding into biological weapons research just after the National Science Advisory Board for Biosecurity advised additional scrutiny and just before Donald Trump took office? A big clue may appear in the fact that the recommendation for reauthorization came from Holdren, the population-control zealot working with the Communist Chinese on "gain-of-function research" and "gene editing."

Was Obama trying to create a pandemic to stop Donald Trump? That is an explosive question, but I am not the only one asking it.

Bradman's June 5, 2021, article is titled "Interesting Timing— Obama Administration Lifted Block on 'Gain of Function Research' Just Eleven Days Before President Trump Took Office, January 9, 2017." "This discovery makes the suspicions of an intentionally released pandemic virus, with a political intent, to 'STOP TRUMP' look exponentially more plausible," he wrote. "With people beginning to recognize that U.S. government officials and the intelligence community have been less than honest, and in some cases downright lying, surrounding the origin of the SARS-CoV-2 virus; and when we overlay the political motives in the background of mass narrative deflection from media and other institutions; and when we consider the known lengths that people inside the U.S. government were willing to go in their efforts to eliminate President Trump; discovering that President Obama's administration technically authorized the restart of 'gain of function' research (biological weaponization of SARS virus) just days before President Trump took office is way more than alarming. … Perhaps not a *smoking gun of intent*, but definitely *bloody footprints* walking out the door—in Obama's size" (emphasis his). I STRONGLY SUGGEST THAT YOU READ THIS PARAGRAPH AGAIN!

John Holdren resigned as director of the Office of Science and Technology the day President Trump took office. He later accepted a position as a visiting distinguished professor at Tsinghua University in Beijing. He was likely able to continue collaborating with Chinese scientists during the Trump years, unhindered by American biotechnology laws.

A NEW VIRUS

Throughout the Trump administration, government scientists like Anthony Fauci continued collaborating with Chinese

Communist scientists to engineer potential pandemic pathogens. And we have strong evidence that, at some point, they succeeded: A new virus gained function.

In a *Wall Street Journal* editorial, "The Science Suggests a Wuhan Lab Leak" (June 6, 2021), Dr. Steven Quay and Richard Muller described how this research was likely accomplished. Though the public was focusing on circumstantial evidence, they wrote that "the most compelling reason to favor the lab-leak hypothesis is firmly based in science. In particular, consider the genetic fingerprint of CoV-2, the novel coronavirus responsible for the disease COVID-19. In gain-of-function research, a microbiologist can increase the lethality of a coronavirus enormously by splicing a special sequence into its genome at a prime location. Doing this leaves no trace of manipulation. But it alters the virus spike protein, rendering it easier for the virus to inject genetic material into the victim cell. Since 1992, there have been at least 11 separate experiments adding a special sequence to the same location. The end result has always been supercharged viruses. ... At the minimum, this fact—that the coronavirus, with all its random possibilities, took the rare and unnatural combination used by human researchers—implies that the leading theory for the origin of the coronavirus must be laboratory escape."

An intelligence report compiled by the Minority Staff of the U.S. House of Representatives Foreign Affairs Committee concluded that "the preponderance of evidence suggests SARS-CoV-2 was accidentally released from a Wuhan Institute of Virology laboratory sometime prior to September 12, 2019." Yet the Obama administration well knew about the inadequate safety practices at the Wuhan lab. There were serious red flags all over this high-stakes facility! But NO ONE DID ANYTHING ABOUT THE WARNINGS.

Then in November 2019, a mysterious disease struck a 55-year-old resident in Hubei province, in or near its capital city, Wuhan. This was the first confirmed case of COVID-19.

A GREAT COVER-UP

As viral infections spread in Wuhan, many people immediately asked about the Wuhan Institute. One of them was President Trump. Leftist politicians and journalists quickly labeled such questions unscientific, conspiratorial and even racist.

Yet it is now well established that in the early days of the coronavirus outbreak, the Chinese Communist Party deliberately suppressed reports about the outbreak and even destroyed evidence of it. Rather than trying to contain the outbreak, THE CHINESE NATIONAL HEALTH COMMISSION ORDERED INSTITUTIONS NOT TO PUBLISH ANYTHING ABOUT THE "UNKNOWN DISEASE." By the time they publicized anything, IT HAD ALREADY SPREAD AROUND THE WORLD.

E-mails from that time show that Dr. Fauci was well aware it could have been man-made, and some scientists he was working with knew this. He and his associates also e-mailed each other news reports about the lab-leak theory. But publicly, Fauci insisted that "the science" showed COVID-19 had almost certainly spread to humans from wild bats.

News and social media executives and their journalists attacked and even censored and banned people who spoke of the lab-leak theory. A statement in the *Lancet* signed by 27 public health scientists in February 2020 captures the gist of the prevailing narrative: "We sign this statement in solidarity with all scientists and health professionals in China who continue to save lives and protect global health during the challenge of the COVID-19 outbreak. We are all in this together, with our Chinese counterparts in the forefront, against this new viral threat. ... We stand together to strongly condemn conspiracy theories suggesting that COVID-19 does not have a natural origin."

Why the discrepancy between their private communications and the message to the public? Why the censorship of views that actually aligned with the private observations of Dr. Fauci and other scientists?

It later emerged in National Institutes of Health (NIH)

testimony to Congress that U.S. health officials "eliminated from public view" the genomic sequences of COVID-19 at the request of Chinese Communist Party officials.

THE COMMUNISTS COVERED UP THE VIRUS'S TRUE ORIGINS AND TURNED WHAT SHOULD HAVE BEEN A LOCAL OUTBREAK INTO A GLOBAL PANDEMIC. We must take seriously the theory that all of this was deliberate. We cannot simply push it aside. THIS IS THE COMMUNIST PARTY OF CHINA WE ARE TALKING ABOUT. IT IS TRYING TO GET CONTROL OF THE WORLD. AND THE OBAMA ADMINISTRATION IS GIVING IT A LOT OF HELP.

CENSORING DISSENT

Dr. Francis Collins is another man who helped Barack Obama and the Chinese Communist Party conceal the origins of COVID-19. After Collins led an international effort to map the human genome, Obama made him director of the NIH. As director, Collins supervised Fauci and 6,000 other research scientists. And like many other Obama nominees, he had no qualms about working with Chinese Communist Party scientists.

Dr. Collins serves on the advisory board of a conference sponsored by BGI Genomics, a Chinese military-linked genomics firm. He also met with Prof. Cao Xuetao to discuss areas of collaboration between the NIH and the Chinese Academy of Medical Sciences. These Communist connections make it likely that Dr. Collins was a prime mover in the campaign to shut down the lab-leak theory.

Early in the pandemic, scientists such as Dr. Michael Farzan, Dr. Robert Garry and Dr. Andrew Rambaut observed that the coronavirus had a "furin cleavage site" that suggested gain-of-function engineering. They presented their findings during a February 1, 2020, conference call of experts and sent the notes to Dr. Collins and Dr. Fauci. Collins dismissed the idea of a lab leak as "outrageous," while Fauci said COVID-19 "could not have been artificially or deliberately manipulated." Yet both men lacked enough confidence in their proof to allow a scientific debate over the lab-leak hypothesis merits. Instead, they worked together to silence dissenting voices.

E-mails later released through a Freedom of Information Act request filed by the American Institute for Economic Research revealed that Collins tried to push back against reporting from Fox News' Bret Baier on the lab-leak theory. On April 16, 2020, Collins asked Fauci, "Wondering if there is something NIH can do to help put down this very destructive conspiracy, with what seems to be growing momentum. ... Ask the National Academy to weigh in?" Fauci replied, "I would not do anything about this right now. It is a shiny object that will go away in time." But he still worked to discredit those exposing the lab leak. In fact, Dr. Peter Daszak, a U.S. researcher with close ties to the Wuhan lab, thanked Fauci in an April 18, 2020, e-mail for "publicly standing up and stating that the scientific evidence supports a natural origin for COVID-19 from a bat-to-human spillover, not a lab release from the Wuhan Institute of Virology."

Other e-mails show that Collins and Fauci also worked to suppress the Great Barrington Declaration, a statement by Harvard's Martin Kulldorff, Oxford's Sunetra Gupta and Stanford's Jayanta Bhattacharya against blanket pandemic lockdowns. These three favored a policy that would not decimate the U.S. economy and would focus only on high-risk populations such as the elderly or those with medical conditions. Thousands of scientists signed this declaration, but Collins condemned its authors as "three fringe epidemiologists." Fauci sanctimoniously proclaimed that those who criticize him are "really criticizing science, because I represent science. It's dangerous."

The lengths to which Collins and Fauci went to convince people that COVID-19 originated naturally and that blanket lockdowns were necessary, and to silence dissenting voices even from prominent scientists, show they were more interested in hiding their role in financing Communist Chinese gain-of-function research than in helping their nation!

SUSPICIOUS TIMING

Dozens of government officials knew about what was really happening in Wuhan, but none of them leaked any information to the public. Some may have been too afraid to say anything, knowing how powerful and vindictive Obama is. But many Obama-era officials were Communists themselves, people who *wanted* to use the fear of a virus to justify draconian, unconstitutional lockdowns.

These measures vastly increased the power of the state at the expense of individual freedoms. This was not an unfortunate, unavoidable by-product. This was the goal! The measures provided authorities who dislike the Constitution's limitations on governmental interference a weapon to push aside those limitations and force their will on the public. They empowered them to ignore the law and to rule by their own whims. And all this was abetted by a supportive, leftist media and by major tech companies that suppressed all contrary views. *This was not about the science!*

JOHNS HOPKINS UNIVERSITY RESEARCH IN FEBRUARY 2022 FOUND THAT PANDEMIC LOCKDOWNS PREVENTED ONLY 0.2 PERCENT OF COVID-19 DEATHS! But saving lives was never the radical left's goal. The goal was to use the pandemic to frighten people into surrendering their God-given freedoms.

Very importantly, drastic government actions made possible only by coronavirus fears revolutionized elections in America. The push for mail-in balloting and other loosening of or illegally breaking long-standing election standards that protect against fraud could only have happened by heavily marketed virus fears. COVID-19 enabled the Democratic Party to field a presidential candidate who could not endure the rigors of a national campaign and who electioneered through Zoom calls from his basement. COVID-19 made it possible for Joe Biden to host a limited number of "rallies" attended by handpicked individuals seated in sparse numbers of chairs spaced far apart from each other. COVID-19 guaranteed a historically bizarre campaign and

UNPRECEDENTED ELECTION THAT INSTALLED BARACK OBAMA'S CHOICE FOR PRESIDENT IN THE WHITE HOUSE.

The timing of all these events is deeply suspicious. Obama's support for the Chinese Communist Party's Wuhan Institute of Virology and its bioweapons research is either the result of horrendous incompetence or diabolical treason. THE BIBLE INDICATES TREASON!

BARACK OBAMA CAME TO POWER BY PRETENDING HE WAS A MODERATE SOCIAL DEMOCRAT, BUT HIS GOAL IS TO FUNDAMENTALLY TRANSFORM AMERICA INTO SOMETHING WORSE THAN A COMMUNIST DICTATORSHIP.

The late Herbert W. Armstrong warned America decades ago that *"the Communist Party* is NOT a mere *political party,* in the sense Americans think of the term. *It is a ruthless totalitarian dictatorship.* It is run, with absolute power, by a few men at the top—all of whom are completely subservient to one man who is Dictator Absolute. This one-man dictatorship is supposed to be necessary because there may be different *interpretations* of the Marxist philosophy. Therefore, to prevent division, they must have a supreme INTERPRETER" (*Plain Truth,* February 1962). Obama, who was mentored by the card-carrying Communist Frank Marshall Davis, wants to be the supreme interpreter of American communism. Toward this end, the coronavirus has become his most dangerous weapon for convincing people to abandon constitutional freedoms and embrace authoritarian government.

The pandemic, its coverage, the government's radical reaction to it, and the election that was altered by it trace back to a man with the stated agenda of "fundamentally transforming the United States of America" and blotting out the blessings and traditions of this country!

GLOSSARY AND INDEX

campaign, Joffe and media outlets to gather and disseminate anti-Trump accusations from Steele, along with illegally obtained and misleading Internet data from Joffe; lied to FBI General Counsel that he was not working for the Clinton campaign and billed the Clinton campaign for the conversation: 74-75, 78

Trump, Donald *President of the U.S. (Jan. 2017 to Jan. 2021); motivated to "make America great again"; reversed transformation of U.S.:* 50-59; *corollary to King Jeroboam II:* 52-59; *main target of Obama*

Wright, Jeremiah *Radical pastor of church in Chicago, which Obama attended for years:* 15, 18-19

Yates, Sally *Deputy attorney general (Jan. 2015 to Jan. 2017); present at Jan. 5, 2017, Oval Office meeting and the second, smaller meeting that day; signed two FISA court applications to spy on Carter Page and the Trump campaign:* 65, 97, 100

YOUR PART

You recognize that America is under attack. But how can you possibly fight back?

Donate to a party? Volunteer in a campaign? Vote in an election? Pass a new law? Secure additional funding?

Washington, Adams, Jefferson, Madison, Lincoln, Reagan and other Americans knew that the future of a nation depends on its character, and the character of a nation depends on each person within it. You are not a spectator in history. You are a participant.

Learn what you can do. Learn what you must change. Face the evils that affect not just your country but your life. One book, perhaps more than any other, can help you start. Request your free copy of *How to Be an Overcomer*.

THIS HAS HAPPENED BEFORE

The attack on America is unprecedented. Never before has someone professed to be loyal to this country, taken its most powerful office, and used that power and the indifference of the people to destroy this country's principles and ideals.

It is unheard-of nationally—but this exact sequence of events has already happened in God's true Church.

These two attacks are connected. They are ultimately directed against the same target, and they ultimately come from the same source.

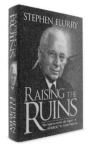

Prove this bold claim by comparing your own Bible to *Raising the Ruins*. This book documents the life-and-death struggle of God's Church in our lifetimes, and leads you directly to the source for understanding physical Israel (America and related nations) and spiritual Israel (the one true Church).

CONTACT INFORMATION

To reach the Philadelphia Church of God to order
literature or to request a visit from one of God's ministers:

MAILING ADDRESSES WORLDWIDE

UNITED STATES: Philadelphia Church of God
P.O. Box 3700, Edmond, OK 73083

CANADA: Philadelphia Church of God
P.O. Box 400, Campbellville, ON LOP 1B0

CARIBBEAN: Philadelphia Church of God
P.O. Box 2237, Chaguanas, Trinidad, W.I.

BRITAIN, EUROPE AND MIDDLE EAST:
Philadelphia Church of God, P.O. Box 16945
Henley-in-Arden, B95 8BH, United Kingdom

AFRICA: Philadelphia Church of God
Postnet Box 219, Private Bag X10010, Edenvale, 1610

AUSTRALIA, THE PACIFIC ISLES, INDIA AND SRI LANKA:
Philadelphia Church of God
P.O. Box 293, Archerfield, QLD 4108, Australia

NEW ZEALAND: Philadelphia Church of God
P.O. Box 6088, Glenview, Hamilton 3246

PHILIPPINES: Philadelphia Church of God
P.O. Box 52143, Angeles City Post Office, 2009 Pampanga

LATIN AMERICA: Philadelphia Church of God, Attn: Spanish
P.O. Box 3700, Edmond, OK 73083 United States

WEBSITES

PHILADELPHIA CHURCH OF GOD: pcg.church
THE TRUMPET: theTrumpet.com
ARMSTRONG INTERNATIONAL CULTURAL FOUNDATION: Armstrong.Foundation
HERBERT W. ARMSTRONG COLLEGE: HWACollege.org

CONNECT WITH US

E-MAIL: letters@pcog.org
FACEBOOK: facebook.com/PhiladelphiaChurchofGod
TWITTER: @PCG_News